One Brain
Change Your Mind

"My Opportunity"
My Story

Chelle~ Blessed to call you my Friend!

Love & Hugs

Written by: Deb Lewin

Deb Lewin

For More Information Contact:

Whitehall Publishing
P.O. Box 548
Yellville, AR 72687
www.whitehallpublishing.com
info@whitehallpublishing.com

Deb Lewin
www.DebLewin.com
RideStrong@aol.com

Printed in the U.S.A.
Retail Price: $14.95

Publisher's Note

You might notice that there are some unusual spellings for words. Please note that these are the common British English spellings for the same words. Deb Lewin was born, raised and educated in Rhodesia, Africa, in a country that was then a British colony, so we felt it appropriate to reflect that in her spelling and use of slang.

Dad took this picture of me loving my first puppy. *Rhodesia*

Dedication

I dedicate this book, with my greatest love and admiration, to the memories of my amazing parents, Margaret & John Lewin.
I love and miss you both more than you will ever know.

Thank you Mom for loving me unconditionally. Thank you for being that shoulder I could always lean on and for always being there to ask me how my day was. Thank you for teaching me that cooking with love and sharing meals always makes food taste better, especially your amazing egg sandwiches. Thank you for instilling in me the values of volunteering and always helping others, for reaching down to raise someone else up. Thank you for sharing with me your great communication skills which have nurtured lifelong friendships.

Thank you Dad for loving me unconditionally. Thank you for your sound advice on maintaining a positive outlook on life and practicing the art of being respectful and grateful. Thank you for encouraging me to play sports, to be a competitive athlete and for teaching me the value of great sportsmanship! Thank you also for sharing your perspective with me on the useless art of worrying – *worrying is like a hamster running on a wheel; it is exhausting and gets you nowhere!*

Dad, Mom and I on our final cruise together. *Alaska*

In Memory of Mikey -
My Brother, My Friend

In memory of my courageous and brave brother Mikey, who passed away in the summer of 2014 at the young age of 63, due to complications from a 42-year battle with diabetes.

Mikey - You were a very talented musician and our family evenings of singing and playing musical instruments will be a blessed memory, stored safely in my heart forever. Your great sense of humour always put a smile on my face.

I thought I was a perfectionist until we worked together in the video industry where I realized I was a mere amateur compared to your pursuit of perfectionism.

Thank you for the deep love and respect you showed to our family and to all our friends. I love and miss you so much Mikey and I thank you for being my precious brother and such a "Mensch" in this world.

Mensch - A Yiddish word meaning
"A person of integrity and honour."

Mikey and Deb celebrating his 60th birthday. *Texas*

My heartfelt love, endless gratitude and a
Texas size THANK YOU to Tammy for loving me
unconditionally, encouraging and supporting me.
You are my soul mate and I thank you for always
being by my side and believing in me.

Special hugs to our precious fur-babies
Bosque, Cowboy and Max.

To my brothers Trev, Rob and sister-in-law Joy, to my amazing
family and extended family of friends, my gratitude and
appreciation for your kindness, thoughtfulness, love, support
and continuous encouragement. Thanks Y'all.

This book would not have been published without the patience,
talent and support of Bonnie from Whitehall Publishing.
Thank you Bonnie!

~

A portion of the profits from the sale of this book will be donated
to Equest Therapeutic Horsemanship in Wylie, Texas. Equest is a
non-profit organization that offers equine assisted therapy to
children and adults with physical and mental disabilities as well as
equine programmes for Veterans and their families.

The monies donated will go towards the Deb Lewin
Scholarship fund. This scholarship programme offers financial
assistance to current Equest riders to help offset the expenses
associated with participating in horse shows and to assist staff
members towards fees for continuing education.

Humans - Horses – Hope
www.Equest.org

Celebrating Mom's 80th Birthday. (l-r) Mikey, Rob, Trev, Joy, Deb, Mom and Tammy. *Texas*

Table of Contents

Publisher's Note I
Dedication II
In Memory of Mikey IV

Before "My Opportunity" 1
"My Opportunity" 21
It's My Party! 31
EQUEST – A Gift that Keeps on Giving 35
Never Look a Draft Horse in the Mouth 43
Horses Saved my Coffee Cups 47
Patience and Flexibility 49
Neuro-Linguistic Programming (NLP) 53
Goal Reaching 59
From Independent to Totally Dependent 65
Spontaneous 67
Get Creative 71
I Can See Enough to Laugh at Myself 75
Choices – Respond or React 79
Fowl-Play 85
Focus 87
Giving and Receiving Assistance 93
Volunteering – Can You Spare some Change? 97
Wheelchair Etiquette 101
Sense of Humour 107
More Funny True Stories: 109
It is the Thought that Counts 113
Self-Motivation, Trust and Attitude 117
Saddled with Backache to Back in the Saddle 123
We all Know what Assume Does!! 127
Skiing in Aspen – This is How I Roll 129
Follow Me Mom 131
Our Shooting Star 135

Table of Contents

Mistaken Identity 139
Fire Drill – Not for us Foreigners! 141
Tales, Straight from the Horses' Mouth 143
I Dream of Africa 151
Openings in Heaven 165
When I Say this ... I Mean this 167
Epilogue 171
About Deb Lewin 173
Order Form 175

Before "My Opportunity"

You are probably wondering about the title of this book - well it is interesting if you think about the many life-changing situations that happen to each and every one of us on a daily basis and yet the most profound for me had to be the brain injury I sustained on February 26th, 1996. It literally **changed my mind!**

I refer to this event in my life as, "My Opportunity."

Before I share the many life-changing experiences I have had since "My Opportunity," let me tell you a little about my past life so that you can better understand where I came from and where I am going.

I was born and raised in Africa, in a country formerly called Rhodesia, now called Zimbabwe, located inland about 1500 miles north from the southernmost point of the African continent. It was a beautiful and extremely prosperous country when I grew up there. It is a small land locked country, about two-thirds the size of the state of Texas and it is bordered by South Africa to the south, Mozambique to the east, Zambia to the northwest and Botswana to the southwest. I was born in the city of Salisbury, now known as Harare.

Deb at 18 months. *Rhodesia*

There are many amazing sights to see in such a small country. Zimbabwe has the largest man-made lake in the world called Lake Kariba, which is more than 140 miles long and about 20 miles wide. By volume, it is the largest artificial lake and reservoir in the world and people come here from all over the world to game fish in these waters for the ferocious tiger fish.

Zimbabwe is also home to one of the Seven Wonders of the World, Victoria Falls also known as Mosi-oa-Tunya (the Smoke that Thunders). It is the largest waterfall in the world and borders Zimbabwe and Zambia on the Zambezi River. It is made up of five different "falls," four of these are on the Zimbabwe side: The Devil's Cataract, Main Falls, Rainbow Falls and Horseshoe Falls with The Eastern Cataract being on the Zambian side. This is not the highest or widest waterfall in the world and yet it is considered the largest waterfall, based on its width of 5604 feet and height of 354 feet, resulting in the world's largest sheet of falling water. It is roughly twice the height of Niagara Falls in America.

My parents, Margaret and John were very well known in Rhodesia. My Dad co-owned several furniture stores ranging from high-end top dollar stores to second-hand furniture stores. He worked hard at building up all these businesses and was very well respected. My Mom was the first woman in Africa to be an account executive in a large advertising company – her first major account being a cigarette company, which was a huge account back then. This kind of work had been reserved for men only. She had broken the stereotype and paved the way for women in advertising and film production.

My parents were loved by so many. They both enjoyed a large circle of friends including the Mayor and Vice President of Rhodesia. They were a very social couple and Mom was often recognized for all the volunteering and fund raising events she did for several non-profit organizations.

We lived in a suburb just north of the capital city of Salisbury, called Mount Pleasant. It was a modest home on about an acre of land with a swimming pool in the backyard. We were a working middle class family and like most other Rhodesians at the time, we were privileged to have servants.

Deb at Junior School. *Rhodesia*

Maudie was our Nanny, Benson was our Cook and Kootch was our Yard guy. All our servants lived on the premises and were treated like part of our family. One of my favourite memories of growing up was being awakened in the morning on school days by Maude, taking a warm bath that she prepared for me each morning then going back into my bedroom to get dressed. Maude laid out my ironed school uniform, my ironed underwear and socks as well as my perfectly shined school regulation shoes each morning. She also tidied my room and made my bed for me. From there, I would join my Dad and brothers in the dining room and we all enjoyed a full breakfast prepared for us by Benson before my Mom drove me to school, in our shiny car freshly cleaned by Kootch. I never knew how spoilt I was until I left Africa and had to learn how to do laundry, cook and clean for myself.

I am a 3rd generation African and I enjoyed a wonderful youth and all of my teen years, growing up in this amazing country with my parents and four older brothers. I was surrounded by my grandparents, lots of aunts, uncles and cousins and numerous friends. Our house was the go-to house for all our friends. We would often get together to share special occasions or just hang out by the pool and enjoy a day of sun, fun and lots of delicious food on the braai (BBQ). What treasured memories I have of these big family gatherings, especially times spent out of town at Auntie Lila and Uncle Salvo's farm.

For half my life in Rhodesia, we were considered a British colony. This comes attached to a strict upbringing, regimented schooling including wearing school uniforms, and irreproachable good manners. The climate and terrific weather allowed us to spend most of our spare time playing outdoors. Sports were always a major part of our childhood. My brother Stan played rugby for Rhodesia and I was able to represent my high school and later my country of Rhodesia in field hockey as the goalkeeper! During my short time on this team, we never played any international competitions because of restrictions and sanctions against my country. After I moved away and the country changed its name to Zimbabwe, my friends got to compete at the Olympic Games in Russia.

When I was almost 20, the political unrest in my country was escalating. Military service for the guys was mandatory, immediately after finishing high school, followed by many stints in the bush every year thereafter. These stints in the bush started off as one month a year and continued to increase in length and frequency. By now, the war was so bad that my soon-to-be husband Bryan and my brothers were continually serving six weeks in the military then six weeks home to continue their regular employment and family life. It was an unbearable time for everyone as reintegration back and forth between military life and civilian life was not happening in just six weeks. This was having a negative effect on all the soldiers, their families and employers.

It was at this time, that Bryan and I, just newlyweds, together with my parents, brothers Trev and Rob, his wife Joy and son Craig, who is also my G-D son, decided to move together to Israel. My older brother Mike, his wife Tiki and their daughter Michelle had already moved to the states where my youngest niece Monique was later born.

Coming from Rhodesia, a country on whom worldwide sanctions had been placed, we had very few choices when it came to emigrating from our homeland. When we made our decision to leave the country, we told our family of our plans to emigrate and yet to everyone else, we made it look like we were going on a holiday (vacation), by purchasing return trip (round trip) flight tickets and placing all our belongings into storage.

The one country that welcomed us and encouraged us to become new immigrants was the young state of Israel. As a Jewish family, we were welcomed into this 30-year-old country through a process called "Aliyah" meaning to ascent or return to the Holy Land. Israel is a very small country, only 240 miles long and about 10 miles wide at its narrowest point.

Moving away from our family and friends, to a foreign country with a very foreign language, took its toll on all of us. We left Rhodesia with a couple of suitcases and very little money. The Rhodesian Government regulated the amount of foreign currency each family could have when travelling and this very small amount was recorded in your passport and sold to you at the bank, upon proof of your travel itinerary and flight tickets. The Rhodesian Dollar had no value outside of Rhodesia and it was illegal to buy or keep any foreign currency.

For our first six months, we lived in a city called Ashkelon, located on the coast in the southern area of Israel, about 35 miles south of the capital city, Tel Aviv. We lived in special high-rise buildings, which were subsidized by the government for new immigrants only. The apartments were furnished with very basic essentials like a stove, fridge, kitchen table and chairs. We were also given bedding, some pots and pans and a few pieces of cutlery. We met so many Jewish people from all over the world that were making "Aliyah" to Israel, for so many various political or personal reasons.

While living here, we all attended school six days a week to learn our new language of Hebrew. Initially it was fun and exciting sitting next to my parents in a classroom, learning the Hebrew alphabet – then reality set in. My parents were at that stage in their lives when they should have been thinking about retiring, not about starting all over again with nothing!

It was a very hard life for all of us and we struggled to integrate into our new country as we learnt to speak, read and write Hebrew! We all had to work several full time jobs just to make enough money to pay rent and have a little food on the table. The work week in Israel is six days, starting on Sunday morning and finishing at around 3pm on Friday, closing for the Sabbath with shops and public transport starting up again after sunset on Saturday.

I worked for a mortgage company from 8 am till 3 pm, six days a week, followed by three to four hours a day working at an ice cream parlour and finishing up every evening working in a British pub as a waitress till 1 or 2 in the morning. I would get a couple of hours sleep and start it all again. I was young and active so I could handle the lack of sleep and long gruelling hours. I did what needed to be done to survive.

Being an athlete and avid sports lover, my refuge in Israel was playing sports. This allowed me an opportunity to meet new people, make some life-long friends and start living a different life. It was not long before I was representing the country of Israel in international competition in both field hockey and squash (similar to American racquetball). We got to play a lot of international games culminating in the Maccabiah Games (Jewish Olympics), which lasted about two weeks in Israel. The opening and closing ceremonies are very similar to the Olympics and athletes from all over the world get to participate. I can still feel the adrenalin rush surging through my body as I walked into the crowded stadium with all the athletes, coaches and members of the Israeli team. This was a once in a lifetime experience.

I loved the food in Israel and I sure do miss it. There were lots of restaurants and little food vendors on the street corners, selling fresh hot pita bread with my favourite stuffing of falafel, hummus, tehina, salad, pickled vegetables and hot sauce. Falafel is a deep-fried ball made from ground chickpeas/ garbanzo beans. Hummus and tehina are sauces made from chickpeas and roasted sesame seeds, lemons, olive oil and other spices. It was encouraged and

Playing goalie was my favourite position in field hockey. *Israel*

accepted to walk along the streets and the beaches eating your fresh culinary purchases.

Although the language barrier and the extreme inflation in Israel made living there a daily battle, the day-to-day energy of the Israeli people and their unshakable zest for living life to the maximum, helped me enjoy the three years I lived in the Middle East. While living in Israel, we were blessed with the birth of my youngest nephew, Adam.

Almost three years after arriving in Israel, Bryan and I got divorced. We had both changed so much in that short time and we fully realized that our goals and desires were not running in the same direction. I loved Bryan as a friend, a brother yet not as a husband. The traditional expected role of a wife, was not who I was.

I knew I was different! There was a knowing in my heart that I was born different. I thought I was gay and yet there were no support groups or accessible information to help me identify these feelings. Being gay was considered a mental issue. It was considered a defiant act against normal societal behaviour. It was wrong, plain and simple. This was all I had to go on with my strict British upbringing, Jewish roots and the pressure from my family to be "normal."

It took several years for me to accept myself. I was always worried about hurting my parents' feelings and causing issues for my family. My parents never stopped loving me. Initially, they thought it was their fault, especially my mother, who felt like she had done something very wrong. Then they attempted to "talk me out of being gay" by making me go with them on several appointments, to see a psychotherapist. When they too realized that I was born like this, and they could see how happy I was in myself, they were very accepting of me and my friends.

I returned home to Africa, to my country with yet another name change, now called Rhodesia-Zimbabwe. There I lived with my second set of parents, Auntie Lila and Uncle Salvo for about a year. By then, my oldest brother Stan, his wife Sheila and their two children, Darienne and Nathan, had moved about 1300 miles away to South Africa, to live in Cape Town, near Auntie Lil and her family. My dearest cousins Fortunee (Twinny) and Linda (Nonees), who were more like my sisters, had also left the country.

I loved being back home, spending time with my grandparents, affectionately known by me as Sunshine and Grumpy. I so enjoyed being with my best friends from school, Sonia and Dazie and visiting all the familiar places I had missed so much. My *soul batteries* were being recharged by the sounds and smells of Africa, especially during the rainstorms and my taste buds were in ecstasy, eating all my favourite foods that are not available anywhere else in the world. Oh, my heart was so full again by being back in Africa.

I had been home less than a year before my precious Grumpy passed away. A few months later, I moved 600 miles south to live in the country of South Africa. I lived and worked in the major city of Johannesburg, commonly referred to as Jo'burg. As much as I was ecstatic about being back in Africa, the travel bug had bitten me once again! It was here in Jo'burg that Helen and I met through mutual friends. We had a lot of friends in common and yet had not met each other until then. Helen was a free-spirited artist. She was very talented and lived life to the fullest.

So, after a few years of working in Jo'burg and saving money, Helen and I took off for Europe via Israel. We spent several months with my parents in Israel and travelled from Haifa in the north to Sharm el-Sheikh (now part of Egypt) in the south. Some of the highlights were floating on the Dead Sea, visiting the city of Jerusalem, the Arab market, walking through the ancient port city of Jaffa, the beaches and the amazing city of Tel Aviv. We made some good friends in Israel and have stayed in contact with several people through the years. One of my dearest friends, Pash now lives in Oklahoma City and we connect on a regular basis.

From Israel, we continued our travels by catching a really cheap three-day ride on a ship from Israel to Greece. It was very inexpensive because we slept outside on the top deck with the other backpackers and gypsy travellers, totally isolated from the full fare paying cruise customers. There was only one plastic awning on this deck to keep us semi-sheltered from the rain and the elements - I use the word *semi-sheltered* very sparingly! Theft was a major issue on this deck, so to protect our belongings, Helen and I slept sitting upright, back-to-back with our backpacks on. In retrospect we might have been a little crazy, although that thought never crossed our minds back then. We were young and adventurous and just wanted to see the world and experience different cultures. We always felt very safe in our travels.

We backpacked our way thru most of Europe for almost a year on a really tight budget of only one US dollar a day. We slept in tents, train stations, youth hostels and on kitchen floors. We thumbed rides, rode bikes, walked, rode trains and buses and ate day-old bread, fruit and vegetables or whatever we could cook on our super small one pot portable gas cooker.

Some of my favourite countries were: Greece, where we saw the Collosseum and the Parthenon on the Acropolis; Italy, where we got to visit Michelangelo's Statue of David and spend some time in the romantic city of Venice; Germany, where we met some amazing people in Hamburg and got to stay in the home of our new friend Pomfritz Kristin for many weeks. I loved the automated kiosks at the German train stations, which served hot chips (French fries) with fresh chopped onion and mayonnaise on it; Austria, where we took a ferry ride on the Danube river, the second largest river in Europe; Switzerland for its picture perfect clean streets and towns; Holland for its windmills and adult entertainment in the red light district and then England, where we stayed with some African friends and thoroughly enjoyed visiting Buckingham Palace, Big Ben, London Bridge over the Thames river and the many museums and galleries, *a few too many for my liking,* We also got to frequent a lot of British pubs with each place having its own special ambience.

Then, it was time to make our final backpacking destination to the USA to see my family in Texas, before returning back to South Africa.

Our first entry into the USA was through New York, so we spent the weekend with my mom's first cousins, Stan and Kathleen and their children Robert, Brenda, Danny, little Kathy and Val in Queens, Long Island. From there, we flew south to Texas to stay with my family in a city about 15 miles north of Dallas, called Richardson.

I must add something here about our New York cousins. We had no idea that we even had family in the USA. My grandmother's brother had moved from Africa when he was very young (before my time) and no one stayed in touch with him so we had no idea where he was. It was not until the mid-1970s that our families made contact and they came over from New York to meet us in Africa. What a blessing this was! We have all remained in close contact since then.

When we arrived in Richardson, we were lucky enough to stay with my brother Rob, Joy and their two sons for the first couple of months and then we moved in with my brother Mike, Tiki and their two daughters for another couple of weeks. With only $100 to my name and a well-worn backpack, I found out very quickly that we could not hitch hike or thumb rides on the Texas highways, as it was not legal or safe. Also, the cost of trains and flights to travel elsewhere were prohibitive, given my lack of finances. I thought I was educated about the size of America, yet I truly had no concept of the magnitude of this country – it is huge! So, pop went my uneducated idea of backpacking around the states by the method of two good legs and a thumb to hitch rides.

My $100 dwindled away very quickly. In fact, almost half of it went on a taxi ride from Dallas back to Richardson. Helen and I got a ride into downtown Dallas to see all the sights and explore the city. We had experienced such amazing bus, train and underground public transport in all the other countries and cities we had visited that we assumed the same to be true in Dallas. We had a wonderful day in Dallas and as daylight was fading fast, we asked all the locals where we could catch a train or bus back to Richardson. We were laughed at a lot, as there was no public transport that went to Richardson from Dallas. We had to get a taxi back to our house and this cost us almost $50. I know we were taken for a ride, both literally and figuratively.

Not long after I arrived in Texas, my home country in Africa changed its name again, this time to Zimbabwe. So here I was in the USA with my only form of identification being my Rhodesian passport – a passport no longer recognized, as the country did not exist anymore!

Even though I was born and raised in Rhodesia, as were many of my immediate family before me, we were not granted automatic Zimbabwe citizenship.

It was at this time that my family in Texas helped me apply for residency in the USA. I already had a lot of family here in Richardson; my two brothers Mike and Rob and their families, my biological father Sol and his wife Laureen, and several younger half brothers and sisters; Tony, Sam, Derrick, Grant, Owen and Fleur. My brother Stan and half-sister Mandy still lived in South Africa. Not long after I arrived here, my Mom, Dad and brother Trev came from Israel to live in Richardson as well.

The immigration process was an interesting and scary one for me with the Immigration and Naturalization Services (INS) having so much power. I remember going several times to get in the queue (line) to see an INS agent. These queues were very, very long and wound all around the uncovered parking lot. Often we would get there four hours before the INS office would open and wait patiently in the queue, through rain and windy conditions, only to get to the entrance and be told to come back the following week, as the day's quota had been filled already! There were certain days designated to each country for immigration services. It took over six weeks of visits to the INS offices to finally get my application submitted.

For the next several months I was very nervous, not knowing if I would be granted residency here in the United States and not having a valid passport to travel elsewhere. During this uncertain time, I alternated my living arrangements between my brothers Mike, Rob and their families. After a few months, I received my resident alien status and got my green card (which was actually blue in colour.) This allowed me to get a Social Security number, get tested and receive my Texas drivers' licence, drive on the *wrong* side of the road from what I was used to, get employment and open a bank account. Now I could look for a job, get a credit card, get into debt, get a loan to buy a car and live the American Dream. Yee hah – I love this country!

The state of Texas is a right-to-work state. This means under the Texas Labour Code, a person cannot be denied employment because of their membership or non-membership in a labour union or other labour organization. This allowed me to work several jobs simultaneously, without having my work hours or pay regulated and defined by the labour union. I was very active in the video industry as a videographer and editor. While working full time, I went to night school and graduated as an Emergency Medical Technician (EMT) followed by another year of studying to receive my advanced Paramedic certification. I also studied Neuro-

Linguistic Programming and received my Master Practitioner Certification in NLP and became a certified ropes challenge course instructor. My training in NLP took me to Canada, Zimbabwe and South Africa to teach and share this amazing information.

I loved being a Paramedic.
Texas

Even though I was working multiple full time jobs, including part time puppy sitting, baby-sitting and house painting, I would spend what little spare time I had, volunteering and helping others in any way I could. Most of my volunteering was connected to raising money for women in shelters and AIDS related facilities including food pantries. This was done through potluck dinners, sporting events and talent shows to name just a few. I was amazed at the tireless conviction of so many people for so many worthy causes.

After four solid years of working in Texas, Helen and I took our first vacation back home to Zimbabwe and South Africa. On returning to the USA from Africa, I began to understand what it was like to live the American Dream – even though I was working seven days a week and holding down three different jobs, the opportunities appeared endless if you were willing to do what it takes.

We had become very spoilt here in America taking a lot of things for granted: Supermarkets staying open 24 hours a day, 7 days a week; Customer service by phone available mostly 24 hours a day, 7 days a week even after the offices are closed; paying a monthly rate for land line telephones and not paying per minute of conversation; no screaming bomb siren warnings or bomb blasts to feel; abundant choices and sizes of numerous items like cars, mattresses, breads, milks, cheeses, washing powders/liquids, soaps and shampoos etc.; One hour film processing; One hour oil changes for our cars; same day dry cleaning services; drive through banking; fast food; petrol (gas) available on weekends; running water and working electricity every day unless there were specific circumstances preventing that, like an unpredictable lightning hit during a thunder storm or pre-scheduled maintenance for which we are informed of before the event!

I must add here, that initially this abundance of choices available to me in the USA was overwhelming. I would go shopping and when I was faced with all the different milk choices or bread choices, I would just abandon my shopping cart and leave the store very frustrated. Back home, for example, we had one size and one kind of milk and two choices of bread only. It was simple and oddly made everything so easy.

I also feel that we were very blessed growing up in Rhodesia. We had servants so we had our homes cleaned for us, our laundry done for us, our meals cooked for us and our swimming pool, yards and gardens tended to. I also feel like we were spoilt because all petrol (gas) stations, banks and shops closed at noon on a Saturday and did not re-open until Monday morning. This forced us to make our own entertainment, play a lot of sports as well as relax and have quality time with friends and family. The climate in Zimbabwe is one of the best in the world allowing so many outdoor events through most of the year and the meats, vegetables and fruits had no preservatives, no antibiotics and no additives at all, making them so very delicious.

The freedom to travel without military roadblocks and not having to travel in convoy style, was interesting and yet unsettling for me for the first several years of being in the USA. Being able to walk in and out of stores and shops without having every bag searched before entering was also very nice, although I must admit this did take a long time to get used to. Having lived in Rhodesia and then in Israel, I was very used to seeing military vehicles and soldiers carrying guns everywhere. I was accustomed to having my bags and packages searched before entering an office building or store. For me *that* was a feeling of safety. I felt secure surrounded by the military and never once thought of this as a lack of freedom.

It is interesting how my perspective has changed and yet old habits can come back in an instant, even if only temporarily. Tammy and I were in Canada during 9-11. I was on the USA dressage team and we were competing internationally in Vancouver. We decided to stay a couple of extra days after the competition and were due to fly back to Dallas on September 12th. We got the awful tragic news from our families on the morning of September 11th and then we stayed glued to the television. With all the uncertainty, we were scared to go downtown, especially as all the clothing we had was red white and blue with USA flags all over it – we showed our USA pride throughout the dressage competition.

This was a horrendous time for everyone. All flights cancelled, borders closed and we were miles away from our families. Eventually after one week, which felt like a lifetime, the borders opened up again. We were unable to get on any flights out of Vancouver so we decided to drive our rental car over the border to Seattle to catch a connecting flight back home to Texas. This incurred a massive additional charge from the car rental company for taking the car across the border. They charged us four times the regular rate to cross the border just because they could!

When we got to the airport in Seattle, all our bags were opened up and searched and there were military personnel everywhere with guns. My old feeling of security kicked back in and I was very okay with all of this and yet, it freaked Tammy out. She had never experienced this before and it was so very foreign and distressing for her.

My brother Rob with some help from his friend Ken, were able to get us on a flight back to Dallas. Again, this incurred horrendous charges as it was considered a "last-minute" ticket purchase. I was so disgusted that the car rental companies and the airlines were taking such advantage of their customers at a time like this!

It was scary to fly so soon after 9-11 and understandably, it seemed like every passenger on the flight was on high alert and extra sensitive. We were so very glad to touch down in Dallas, see our families and get home to our fur-kids.

Our precious 3 boys: Max, Bosque and Cowboy. *Texas*

So often we take what we have for granted, and fail to appreciate it all until we no longer have it. It is hard to imagine how people in a different country live, until we ourselves have lived there and experienced it first-hand. There is something about us as human beings that feel the need to experience a situation first-hand to learn the lessons, as opposed to learning from someone else's shared experiences.

When Helen and I were almost 30 years old, having lived in the USA for about six years, we had some money saved allowing us to make a down payment on an adorable little house in Richardson. We were able to afford this house, as it was called a "fixer-upper" home. This meant that we had to do a lot of renovations and repairs - pull up all the old stained and cat-pee smelling carpet and replace it, paint the entire house inside and out, replace bathroom walls, tiles and shower doors, fix the garage door so it would close, bring some of the utilities up to code to pass city inspection and cut down old dead trees, just to name a few. This did not matter to us, as we were willing to do the work to own our home.

This was really a fabulous feeling of putting down roots in this great country. I missed Africa so very much and yet my country, as I knew it, was no more! I had to move forward and not spend any more time being a "when-we." *When we* were in Africa, we did this or *when we* were in Africa we had that...

Just before moving into our new home, we got two new family members. Kei, a three-week-old black Labrador that we hand raised, and three weeks later, we got her a puppy to play with - an adorable one-month-old ball of fluff, an Old English sheepdog we called Sagie. These babies were a treasure and a delight and really changed my day-to-day living experiences.

Regardless of what time I finally made it home from one of my many jobs, my fur-babies were always happy to see me, sharing their pure joy and excitement by jumping around, barking and wagging their tails vigorously. This just warmed my heart and always put a smile on my face. They would wag their tails with such enthusiasm and I was always amazed that their tails managed to stay attached to their furry butts, with all that wagging! Kei and Sagie loved unconditionally and were my very best friends. Even though they are both together again playing at the Rainbow bridge, I still miss them very much!

My life was going great - I was learning to speak Texan, which is a language all of its own and I enjoyed all the jobs I had. I continued to play golf, racquetball and learnt how to be a catcher in the American game of softball. I was working out at the gym several times a week to keep fit and I participated in line dancing at the local Country Western clubs. I loved to dance Country Western and I found out that it was true what they said about Country Western music... play it backwards and you do get your wife, kids and pick-up truck back! I also learnt very quickly that cheering for the bull and not the cowboy, at the local rodeo was not acceptable in Texas.

I was slowly integrating into the Texas way of life and yet understanding the game of football is still a challenge for me. I am proud to say though, that I have learnt that a "quarter back" is not a refund and I almost fully understand what it means to "get your bell rung!"

Playing sports allowed me to make many new friends and I had a great social life. When I was not working at one of my many jobs, I was volunteering a lot and spent as much time as I could enjoying Kei & Sagie. Of course, living only a mile away from most of my family was the best part of my new life too!

After nearly eight years as a law abiding, tax paying permanent resident, I applied to become a United States Citizen. I studied American History and passed my citizenship test. Even though I was not permitted to check the box of African American on my immigration application, because I have white skin, I consider myself to be African American. I am third generation African and I now live in America. You can take an African out of Africa and yet you can never take Africa out of an African.

(l-r) Deb, Trev, Stan, Mike and Rob. *Texas*

It was a memorable day when all the new immigrants in Dallas crowded into the courtroom and as they called your name and country of origin, you stood up from your seat and proceeded to meet the judge and get your naturalization certificate and American flag. This allowed me to apply for a USA passport, which I did and it also extended me the privilege to vote, which I did for the first time in my entire life. I am so grateful to be living here in the USA.

I felt like I was living the good-life. I was an independent, healthy able-bodied woman with all the opportunities I could wish for, right in front of me.

Then it happened…

"My Opportunity"

Monday, February 26th, 1996. It was just after 1pm, on a warm, clear blue-skied Texas day and I was driving through Dallas/Fort Worth International Airport, en route to my last job of the day. My day started at sunrise, when I assisted my cameraman to set up equipment for a Soljay Production video shoot with my brother Mike. My second appointment was with Linda V and Kathy, discussing the fine details of an upcoming medical conference that I was going to videotape and edit. My third and final job for the day was at U-Edit video in Arlington, Texas. I was the manager of U-Edit Video in Richardson and often went to help out at the other location.

Suddenly… I was broadsided by another vehicle on my driver's side!

I have a scattered recollection of what happened next - the sound of sirens, metal tearing and glass breaking as I was being cut out of my car by the fire department, my cell phone ringing, not being able to move my body, the distant sound of peoples' voices, the blurred appearance of everything around me and my head throbbing with excruciating pain. The sun was shining and yet I remember shivering and feeling very cold. Everything was in super slow motion and I was told that I drifted in and out of consciousness over the three hours it took for the paramedics and fire department to get me to the trauma hospital.

I had been broadsided by a taxi, driven by a man who was living and working in this country illegally. At the young age of only 36, my life was forever changed. When we started legal proceedings, this taxi driver promptly fled the USA and returned to his home country of Ghana, in Africa. I have never felt any anger, resentment or bitterness towards this driver. Holding a grudge against him was not going to make my situation revert to its original state. I do wish however, that he had gone through the same

21

gruelling immigration process that I did to get into this country legally and obtain all the necessary work permits.

I am a non-believer in accidents – I believe that everything happens for a reason, so I refer to this life-changing event as "My Opportunity."

I sustained a brain injury resulting in left side paralysis, impaired vision, loss of hearing, memory loss and a host of other physical and neurological deficits. I underwent double ear surgery to repair perilymph fistulas caused by trauma. This is a tearing of the small, thin membranes that separate the air-filled middle ear and the fluid-filled space of the inner ear. These holes allowed fluid to leak into my middle ears, so my surgeon had to patch the leaks, to help me with my debilitating headaches and hearing loss. For about three years after this surgery, my mouth stopped producing saliva. My tongue would stick to my gums or roof of my mouth and my lips would stick to my teeth, making it very difficult to talk or to be understood. I often experienced the terrifying feeling of choking due to such a dry mouth and dry throat. This would often make me cough which led to an increase in my asthma attacks. I carried several water bottles with me everywhere I went and had to sip fluids with every mouthful of food so that I could swallow my meals.

I had some cracked vertebrae and bulging discs in my lower back and some damage to my neck. None of these were serious enough to require immediate surgery, although I did end up having to undergo major surgery to both of these areas a few years later. I had an anterior-posterior 360-degree spinal fusion of my lower back with lots of hardware (rods and screws) inserted in my spine and then a few years later, I had a metal plate inserted in my neck during my cervical fusion surgery.

After numerous months of hospitalization, in-patient and out-patient rehabilitation, I was told that I had reached MMI - maximum medical improvement. It was recommended to my family, that they put me in a fully assisted nursing home, as I would probably never do anyting for myself again!

At this point I had been through the gamut of traditional and conventional therapies: Physical and occupational therapy; Pool therapy; Psychotherapy; Speech therapy and even nine months of brain injury school.

Even though I made some great improvements, I still needed assistance 24/7. I needed help with bathing, dressing, cooking, cleaning and of course transportation, just to name a few! I had gone from being a healthy, totally independent, world-travelled, able-bodied athletic woman to a totally dependent woman using a wheelchair.

This brain injury changed my mind. Literally! I found that there were a lot of events and things that I had totally forgotten and then there were events that I only partially remembered and this was so frustrating. I was always in a lot of physical pain and even though I hardly ever complained, this did not make me an easy person to be around. My debilitating pain was being caused by an extremely sensitive head due to the traumatic brain injury which resulted in; severe jaw pain, excruciating headaches and migraines, ear pain from my surgery, neck pain from the bulging disc in my cervical spine, nerve damage to my eyes, unending lower back pain from the fractures and herniated discs and extreme nerve pain in my right hip where the bone was shaved and used in my back fusion surgery. The good news here is that I felt little to no pain on the paralyzed left side of my body.

I had been prescribed several heavy duty narcotic pain medications as well as nerve medications and anti-depressants and yet very little seemed to help me. I was not keen on taking drugs anyway and when I did, the relief was minimal and the side effects were huge. Side effects included:

More memory loss and confusion than I was already experiencing,

Feeling totally disconnected from my surroundings,

More tired and sleepy than I already was with a brain injury,

Heightened frustration,

More extreme focus and concentration problems than I was already dealing with,

More balance problems,

Upset stomach and projectile vomiting,

Extreme sensitivity to light and sounds,

Deeper depression,

Severe anxiety and an overall sense of discomfort and simply not feeling well.

I am very grateful that I did not become addicted to these major narcotics as that would have been just one more issue to add to my long list of *things to get over.*

I sorely lacked the ability to cope with problems or changes to my schedule, which confused me immensely. I was having lots of ups and downs with my emotional state and sadly, the people I would get upset with and "bark" at the most were my closest friends and family who were the same people trying to help me. I was feeling very frustrated and totally useless. Asking for help and needing assistance was a foreign way of life for me and very hard to accept.

Here's a heads up on Traumatic Brain Injuries. I reference the Centers for Disease Control website, www.cdc.gov for the following information and statistics:

"Traumatic brain injury (TBI) is a major cause of death and disability in the United States, contributing to about 30% of all injury deaths. Every day, 138 people in the United States die from injuries that include TBI, that's more than 50,000 people a year. In 2010 about 2.5 million TBI's occurred either as an isolated injury or along with other injuries. Those who survive a TBI can face effects lasting a few days to disabilities which may last the rest of their lives. Effects of TBI can include impaired thinking or memory, movement, sensation (e.g., vision or hearing), or emotional functioning (e.g., personality changes, depression). These issues not only affect individuals, they also have lasting effects on families and communities."

Brain injuries affect the root of who we are - our ability to think, communicate and connect with other people. If you survive a TBI, your life will be significantly affected.

I say it again, **One Brain Injury *will* Change Your Mind.**

It was also at this time that I really found out who my friends were. Those people in my life that I had considered "good friends" were suddenly nowhere to be found—the feedback I would get from them was that it was *too hard for them* to see me in a wheelchair! *Too hard for them…!* Perhaps they would like to be helped out of bed every day and use the wheelchair instead of their legs, and then the true meaning of *"hard for them"* would be appropriate!

As you can imagine, this was a very emotional time and once again, the universe came through for me. I had met some new people, just prior to "My Opportunity," and they showed me their true colours. Among them were Gwapie Jen and my Skippy, true friends in every sense of the word, loving me for who I was and standing side-by-side with me through it all.

So, even though I felt like I was at the end of my rope, the endless love and support of my family and friends allowed me to tie a knot in that rope and hang on. With their encouragement behind me, I was better equipped to face what was in front of me.

They knew me as a determined, motivated individual and an avid athlete. I had represented two different countries in field hockey and squash when I was able-bodied, so they knew I could accomplish my goals and they never stopped pushing me and encouraging me to be the "best me," I could be.

I never asked, "Why me?" through all of this and yet I did think that perhaps my family and friends would be better off if I was no longer on this planet. I felt like I was being a burden, like I was creating additional hardships and pain in their lives.

I had no job. I had no income. My seventeen-year relationship had ended. My medical bills were already in the tens of thousands of dollars with no end in sight. Creditors were relentless in their phone calls and nasty letters.

I could not:

- Hear very well or see much at all,

- Concentrate on anything or hold a single train of thought for any length of time,

- Drive,

- Sit up for too long due to the pain,

- Communicate very well as I thought I knew what I wanted to say and yet I was unable at that time to get my thoughts to match my words or I would use words that made no sense or were completely out of context, even though I thought I was forming them correctly in my mind.

My daily routine consisted of needing help in the following areas:

- A family member or friend entering my house *using their key;*

- Helping me up and out of bed and into my wheelchair;

- Helping me to the bathroom and helping me to transfer onto the toilet seat;

- Helping me to get out of my pyjamas;

- Helping me transfer onto the shower chair;

- Helping me to take a shower, clean my teeth, wash my hair and shave my legs;

- Helping me out of the shower;

- Helping me to dry off my body and dry my hair;

- Pick out my clothes for the day and help me get dressed;

- Helping me back into my wheelchair;

- Helping me to put on my eye patch, neck brace, back brace, arm brace and leg brace;

- Prepare breakfast for me;

- Make sure I took my daily medications;

- Helping me to eat my breakfast;

- Feeding my dogs, Kei and Sagie and filling up their water bowls;

And then each late morning,

- Helping me to remove my eye patch, neck brace, back brace, arm brace and leg brace;

- Helping me out of my wheelchair and back into bed for a nap;

- Leaving my house *with their key* while I slept;

- Another family member or friend entering my house again later in the day *using their key;*

- Helping me up and out of bed again and into my wheelchair;

- Helping me to put on my eye patch, neck brace, back brace, arm brace and leg brace;

- Prepare and help me with lunch;

- Stay with me for a short time while I sat up in my wheelchair and attempted to watch and listen to TV;

- Helping me make doctor's appointments and arrange transport for me;

- Helping me to the bathroom and helping me transfer onto the toilet seat again;

- Helping me back into my wheelchair again;

And then each mid-afternoon,

- Helping me to remove my eye patch, neck brace, back brace, arm brace and leg brace again;

- Helping me out of my wheelchair and back into bed for my afternoon nap;

- Leaving my house again, *with their key* while I slept;

And then each evening,

- Another family member or friend entering my house yet again later in the day *using their key*;

- Helping me up and out of bed yet again and into my wheelchair;

- Helping me to put on my eye patch, neck brace, back brace, arm brace and leg brace for the final time today;

- Helping me to the bathroom and helping me transfer onto the toilet seat once again;

- Helping me back into my wheelchair yet again;

- Helping me roll into the kitchen area;

- Prepare and help me with dinner;

- Helping me get ready for night time, brushing my teeth and hair;

- Helping me change back into my pyjamas;

- Helping me for one final transfer to the toilet for the night;

- Helping me back into my wheelchair again;

- Hanging out for a couple of hours with me;

- Helping me read my mail, stack up my bills, clean my house, wash, dry and fold my laundry;

- Helping me to remove my eye patch, neck brace, back brace, arm brace and leg brace for the final time this day;

- Helping me out of my wheelchair and back into bed yet again;

- Helping me to take all my night time medications;

- Making sure Kei and Sagie had enough treats and water;

- Leaving my house for the final time that day *with their key* while I attempted to sleep through the night;

The next day the same routine – different people and different meals!

This routine changed some when I started going to outpatient therapy several times a week. I was doing a lot of mental and physical exercises in rehab and meeting other patients with challenges to overcome. I still needed all the help I mentioned above, and now I was receiving some of it from the bus drivers that transported me as well as the therapists in the rehabilitation facility.

As I got stronger and stronger, I was able to do some of these things for myself. This encouraged me to want to do more, and by doing more, I was feeling like less of a burden on my family and friends.

Over time, I was able to better control my emotions and had fewer and fewer outbursts. Even though I am still in constant pain, I started to handle it better. The main pain I feel these days is in my back. I get pain shots and nerve block shots in my lower back on a semi regular basis to help with some of this debilitating pain. I also suffer some from headaches and nausea. I still have the constant ringing in my ears which is more frustrating than painful. It also seems that my asthma is getting worse over the years. I think a lot of this has to do with being less active due to the pain in my back. So it is like a domino effect. Yet, I continue to focus on what I can do and just do what I can. As I started to re-learn how to do things for myself, I gained back some confidence and self-respect. I knew I had a long journey ahead of me and I treated every bump on the "road to recovery," with respect and gratitude, holding firm in the knowledge that everything changes in time.

After "My Opportunity," I felt like wonder woman. I would *wonder* where I put my cell phone? I would *wonder* if I closed the door? I would *wonder* if I put the milk back in the fridge and not in the pantry again? My mom always got a good laugh at this wonder woman expression of mine and one day out of the clear blue, she asked me if I believed in the "here-after." I was a little shocked at first and wondered what this was leading up to. She continued to tell me that she was experiencing the "here-after" a lot recently. She would walk into the living room and wonder "what am I *here-after*?" Go into the kitchen and wonder "what I am *here-after*?"

Like mother, like daughter, *wonder woman met the here-after!*

Celene Dion released her single, "Because You Loved Me" on February 19, 1996, just seven days before "My Opportunity." I felt like she wrote this song just for me. The song focuses on thanking those people in your life who were there for you in your darkest hours. It was through "My Opportunity" that I discovered how loved I really am by the people in my own life. That has been an amazing gift for me. I would encourage you to let the people in your life know how much you care about them now, before they become *wonder woman* or start to focus on the *here-after!*

It's My Party!

About 18 months after "My Opportunity," at the age of 38, I continued to get upset and angry about my situation and I would throw my leg brace across the room from sheer frustration. Yes, it felt good for about two seconds and then the frustration set in once again.

I clearly remember the exact negative behaviour I did which made such an impact on me and contributed to the positive path that I have since chosen to travel in my life.

Helen and I purchased our home some seven years earlier, and as I could no longer go *upstairs* to my bedroom, we converted the dining room into my new room. This one particular day I was sitting up in my bed with my wheelchair parked very close to me. I learnt how to transfer myself independently from the bed into my chair and wheel myself around a little bit. Feeling depressed and sorry for myself on this particular day, I was having my own *pity-party for one!*

In my frustration, I reached over to my wheelchair, released the brakes and pushed it away from me. Unaware at that time that the dining room had a slight decline, my chair just took off rolling further and further away from me until it came to a stop in the kitchen. I had taken out my frustration on the one major item that could help me be more independent again. How ridiculous I felt for doing this behaviour and yet my pity-party continued.

Now I was stuck in bed until someone came over to my house to help me and my ego would not allow me to call anyone to come over any sooner than scheduled. This gave me some time to reflect on my behaviour. I suddenly became aware that this challenge could in fact become my greatest blessing. This adversity could elicit some new talents in me that would otherwise have remained dormant.

I had to choose to find the resources I needed to make something special out of "My Opportunity." I was being given another shot at life for a reason, an opportunity to share and encourage others in my situation. So, this began my daily commitment to do whatever I could and whatever I needed to do, to follow my heart and live my purpose.

I also made another conscious decision right then and there. I decided that it was a natural part of my healing journey to get frustrated, so I allowed myself to have a pity-party every now and then, provided I limited my partying time. To me, the major key was not getting too comfortable and staying at the party too long!

Noting when I was heading to that party I would allow myself five minutes of pity-party time. I could rant and rave, cry and perform for that five minutes only, then it was time to move on to more positive and productive behaviours.

Over time, this five minute long pity-party became two minutes and then just a fleeting moment. I can now just wave at the party bus as it races through my mind. That train of thought has left that station.

I am not a religious person, yet I am a very spiritual person. I know that G-D* does not give me more than I can handle – I just wish he didn't trust me so much, to handle so much!

After about a year of living in my makeshift bedroom in the dining room, I was able to move into my wheelchair-accessible, garage-converted, new bedroom. This would not have been possible without the help of so many family and friends worldwide. Even though I had yet to meet my now great friends, Michael and

Bill, they were instrumental in arranging several fund raising events for me as were my Mom, Miri, Esme, Helen, my brother Rob, Glo, Little Christine, Skipper and Cherree, Cindy and Kaye, Chele and Judy, Linda V and Kathy, Jeanne and Lisa, Anna and Tina, Ken and Darla, Barry and Viv, Dr. Pam and Alison, just to name and thank a few! THANKS to everyone involved in donating money, supplies and their time, to convert my garage into a wonderful bedroom.

Helen, being the artist that she is, painted the ceiling of my new room with a beautiful blue sky and white fluffy clouds. Spending so much time in that room, it was magical to look up and get lost in the beauty and magnificence of her talents.

Even though Helen has moved to Colorado, we have maintained our wonderful friendship and we will always be family. I would not be where I am today if it had not been for everything that we went through and for this, I will always be grateful.

* The Jewish religion doesn't necessarily always substitute the letter "o" with a dash in writing the word "G-D" in English. Since G-D is very holy, they may write it hyphenated as a sign of respect, as I also choose to do.

The Deb Lewin Scholarship Fund at Equest.
(l-r back row) Mom, Tammy, Mom Billie, Gail,
(l-r front row) Mom Dot, Deb and Susan. *Texas*

EQUEST - A Gift that Keeps on Giving

About eighteen months after "My Opportunity," my life was once again changed forever. My friend Kim gifted me ten therapy riding lessons at Equest Therapeutic Horsemanship in Wylie, Texas about an hour's drive from my house. Equest, founded in 1981, is a non-profit horse riding facility that offers therapeutic riding to children and adults with physical and mental disabilities, facilitated by specially trained therapists, certified instructors, amazing horses and ever-giving volunteers. In 2012, Equest introduced equine assisted therapeutic programmes for veterans and their families as well.

Prior to receiving this gift, my life-long friend from Israel, Pash, mentioned therapeutic riding to me several times. I had never ridden a horse before and couldn't imagine what benefits I might gain from riding that I hadn't already received from conventional therapies. How could this help me to improve my mental, physical or emotional condition?

Despite my ignorance about all things equine, I was excited about my new adventure. Just the thought of being out of the house and around horses one morning each week, got me willing to "go along for the ride!" I had ridden a camel before and soon found out that this experience was of no benefit to me at all, when it came to being an equestrian! Since learning to ride horses, I have also had the opportunity to ride an elephant in the African bush and some of the same basic principles I learnt from horse riding, applied to riding an elephant.

Lesson One: Mount the horse.

Lesson Two: Stay mounted.

My family and friends set up a transportation roster and took time off from their jobs to get me to Equest every week, especially Laureen, who made it her weekly mission to get me to the barn on time, as well as my numerous transport volunteers in Gail, Tammy, Susan, Beth and Sharon.

The many different emotions I felt on that first day were very confusing. I was afraid and yet being around the horses brought me a sense of peace at the same time. It was wonderful to be wheeled down the aisle of the barn, between the stalls, with all the horses looking over their stall doors to see what was happening. The smell of the hay, the dusty arena and the whinnies from these majestic animals just filled my senses. My first visit to Equest and every visit thereafter filled me with all the emotions on the spectrum... from pure fear to sheer exhilaration! From butterflies in my tummy to goose bumps rising from my nose to my toes. From tears of frustration to tears of joy and accomplishment. What an adventure this was going to be!

Then the fear overtook me again. The therapy horse assigned to me for my first lesson was Mrs. Butterworth, affectionately known as Mrs. B. From my perspective, sitting about three feet high in my wheelchair, with impaired vision and lack of depth perception she looked like a giant! They wanted to put me *up there* - on that little piece of leather called a saddle?

My coach and all my volunteers gently and kindly reassured me. They wheeled me up the ramp and guided Mrs. B beside my wheelchair. Three volunteers helped me into the saddle. Once seated on this little piece of shiny leather on the horse's huge and hairy back, I was more paralyzed from fear than by my injuries. I felt completely out of control. I knew I could not get off by myself, unless I took an "unscheduled dismount."

Even though I have a lot of issues with my memory, I am able to remember a few words that Carol, one of my very first volunteers and now my friend, said to me at my first lesson. I remember looking at her from up on Mrs. B and between tears I said, "This is my first time" and she looked back up at me and in a caring, kind and thoughtful voice she replied, "This is not my first time!" These words are etched in my brain and in my heart.

My first ten lessons were in a group session with five other riders. Caroline was our certified therapeutic riding coach and I needed three volunteers to assist me in the arena. One to lead my horse, Mrs. B and two more volunteers as side-walkers. A side-walker can assist in many different ways and for me, they helped keep my feet in the stirrups and my upper body supported and balanced in the saddle.

I always thought that if the horse was disciplined and well trained, any person could get into the saddle and not have to do much of anything for the horse to perform. Well that bubble was soon burst for me. I had no idea how physically demanding it was to ride a horse.

After my very first lesson on a beautiful, now retired horse named Mrs. B, where I just sat in the saddle and got walked around for about thirty minutes, I was exhausted. I got home that day and slept until noon the next day, just from being on the back of a horse. The next day I had sore muscles in parts of my body that I had not used in a very long time. The movement of the horse was now exercising all my muscles, which were generally only accessed by a person when walking.

When I first started riding, I wore an eye patch, a neck brace, an arm brace, a back brace and a leg brace. After several months, I was making such great progress that I began taking semi-private therapy sports riding lessons and was introduced to my new Equest coach, now my mentor and friend, Gail. After a few more months of riding, I gained more strength in my muscles and was able to get rid of my neck, arm and back braces. Next to go was my eye patch. I finally found a form of therapy that was really working for me.

Gail recognized that my prior, long-dormant athletic spirit could be reignited and she encouraged me to reach a level of riding whereby I could compete against other riders with physical disabilities. It was also at this time that my neuro doctor started to notice the benefits of my equestrian therapy; my paralyzed leg had gained back some muscle, my core stomach muscles and back muscles were stronger, I could hold up my head without a neck brace and my confidence and self-esteem were returning.

Gail got me really involved in the equestrian discipline of dressage and then later into western riding and cart driving. After almost a year of riding different horses at Equest I was invited to participate in a dressage competition in Missouri as a member of the Equest team. We were all assigned borrowed horses, practiced a little and then competed against other riders with similar levels of physical abilities. What a rush this was. I am very competitive by nature and this was the excitement and challenge that my life had been missing. Once again, this confirmed for me that that February day in 1996 was indeed "My Opportunity."

Many of the people I competed against had been riding most of their lives and owned their own horse, affording them the luxury of riding every day. Gail reminded me that it was the journey and not the destination that was important, so even though I only rode once a week, I continued to be the best equestrian I could be, with the horses assigned to me.

I am continually in awe and always delighted with the horses at Equest that can be so gentle and so intuitive. When I get close enough to some of these horses, close enough to feel their warm breath on my face, close enough to stare into their loving eyes, close enough to whisper to them – they speak back to me! Of course, there have been a few that have wanted nothing more than to take a chunk out of me as well.

Most of these horses are smart enough to realize that I have no use of my left leg and arm, so they purposefully step to the left where they know I have to work very hard and use every alternate cue at my disposal to get them to go straight again. This is yet another fantastic lesson I have learnt from these horses.

**Prince took me to another victory
in a western riding competition at Equest.** *Texas*

Some of my all-time favourite horses have been: Mrs B, Taco, Jazz, JJ, Cory, Major, Gingas Khan, Prince, Amigo, Alman, Zeus and Zena. Ranging in ages from seven to twenty-five years old, ranging in height from 14.3 hands up to 16 hands, from 1000 pounds up to 1800 pounds and only one of these was a stallion.

I love this quote by Sir Winston Churchill:

*"There is something about the outside of a horse
that is good for the inside of a (wo)man!"*

Even though I am the one riding and getting so many benefits from Equest, all my family and friends continue to enjoy these benefits as well – this is due to the many positive changes and life lessons that I have taken from riding horses into my everyday life.

-The physical, mental and emotional gains I have experienced from being around and riding horses are numerous and miraculous. Just to name a few that I have experienced:

-Physically, I am stronger, with increased core muscles, better posture, movement and motor skills.

-Mentally, I have improved my ability to communicate both verbally and non-verbally through body movements as well as learning and processing new skills and increased memory functions.

-Emotionally, I am more positive, more optimistic and definitely have more self-confidence. Also, my flexibility, patience and problem solving abilities have improved due to the fact that I would ride different horses at Equest or borrowed horses in competitions and this presented me with different challenges to overcome, each and every time.

I have ridden in outdoor uncovered arenas in minus five-degree wind chill with freezing rain as well as riding and competing in temperatures of over 106 degrees with lots of humidity. I have ridden on backyard, french-fry eating ponies with no arena experience to huge draft horses – each one an amazing experience and a great opportunity, leaving their hoof prints in my heart forever.

One of my all-time favourite Paralympic equestrian events is the musical kur in the discipline of dressage. This is a competition, whereby I get to choose my own music and then choreograph my riding movements to this music. There are several required moves in the test upon which you are judged, including overall composition and fluid changes of riding gaits to the musical tempo and rhythm.

Something that Gail figured out very early in my riding career was that I was able to remember more instructions when it was done with music. Gail would often sing my instructions to me, to the tunes of nursery rhymes. It worked every time. So naturally, the musical kur was my most exhilarating and least stressful of all the events I competed in.

This was also due to the fact that I loved dancing, especially with my Dad. After "My Opportunity" I felt like I had lost my ability to dance anymore, so when I started doing musical kurs, it was as if I was dancing again, this time with the two left and two right feet of the horse.

The horse I rode the most for these events was Zena and she loved to dance as well. Her tail would just swish and she truly felt the beat of the music especially trumpet and big band music. *This just happened to be the music that my Dad and I would dance to most often!* I have since become quite a wheelchair dancer and I thank Tammy and Bobby for always dancing with me and my chair.

Here is a side note about Zena, who was saved from being sent to the meat market when Lee Ann purchased her. She took her up to the highest level that she could in the equestrian discipline of dressage in the able-bodied world and when they could advance no further, and Lee Ann needed to purchase a different horse, she generously donated Zena to Equest. I will be forever grateful to have had the privilege of competing with Zena and ultimately riding in the Olympic stadium in Atlanta, Georgia, during the Paralympic trials. Zena is now trotting around freely in the very green pastures at the Rainbow Bridge.

Riding, being a board member and volunteering at Equest is truly a gift that keeps on giving. Thanks to Ellie, I always have amazing opportunities to share my stories with new volunteers and instructors alike, schools, corporations and other non-profit organizations.

A huge Thank You to Susan, co-founder of Equest, Mom Dot and everyone else involved in the world of equine assisted therapy. I know you are not involved in this profession for the *income*, you are truly involved for the *outcome* and for this I will ALWAYS be grateful. Check out their website at www.Equest.org

The answer to feeling down is to saddle up!

What does it mean if you find a horseshoe?
It means that some horse is walking around in just his socks!

Zena, Deb and Tammy
Dressage high point champions. *Texas*

Never Look a Draft Horse in the Mouth

I remember one particular dressage show I attended in California in 2001 and although ParaEquestrians can now compete on their own horses, it was not like that then. All riders had to compete on borrowed horses that they had not ridden in the previous twelve months!

Dressage is a competitive equestrian sport, where "horse and rider are expected to perform from memory, a series of predetermined movements in each test." Similar to an ice-skating competition, where each mandatory move is scored and the choreography is also taken into consideration by the judges.

We arrived at the barn and I was matched up with two possible horses to compete on. Gail, my coach, rides the horses first to see their responses to my adaptive equipment. One was a definite "no" and the other horse became a "no" after I rode him for a very short time, as there were some safety concerns.

I was so disappointed that we had travelled all the way from Texas to compete in this huge ParaEquestrian qualifying show and I was horseless. The next afternoon, less than a day before we started the competition, this trailer pulled up and out walked one of the largest horses I had ever seen. A stranger in the area heard about my situation and offered me their horse to compete on.

Major, was a 16+ hand Belgium draft horse weighing in at over 1800 pounds, who was trained in the equestrian discipline of vaulting and not dressage. This boy was gigantic and definitely named after his stature. Again, Gail tacked and mounted Major to see his response to my adaptive equipment. Then it was time for me to get up in the saddle. Oh my wordy!! Being only five feet tall and weighing about 105 pounds, I know I looked like a peanut on a mountain. Never the less, I felt blessed that I had a horse to ride and this was certainly going to be a competition I would never forget.

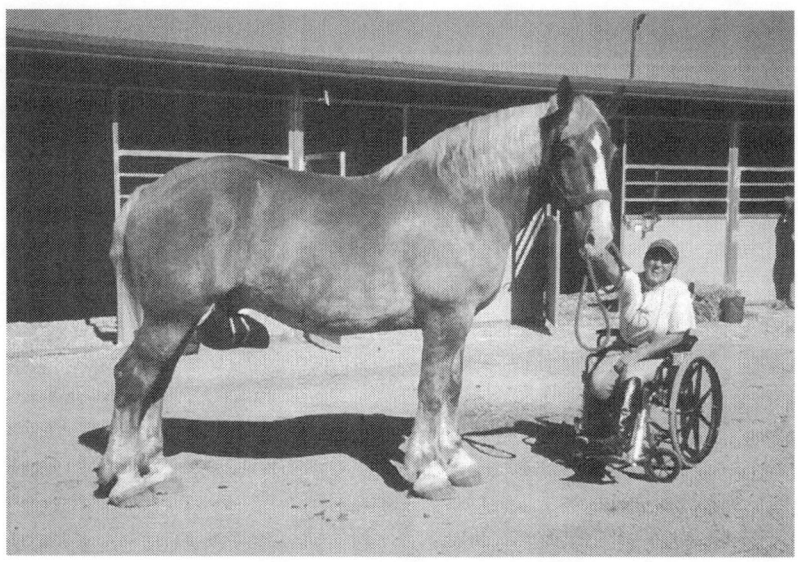

My first heart to heart connection with Major.
California

I got to practice on Major for less than an hour before returning to our hotel to clean my tack and shine my saddle and boots. Just before going to sleep, I followed my normal pre-competition ritual and visualized how I wanted the following day to unravel. I visualized my dressage test and suddenly started laughing out loud. I could visualize Major and I doing many of the required moves on the dressage test; the walk, trot, 20-metre circles and yet when it came to visualizing the 10-metre circles with this 12-metre horse, all I could think about was, where does his head go? I fell asleep with a smile on my face and a knowing in my heart that we would compete and have fun.

Saturday morning, up early and wearing our dressage bests, we headed for the barn. I rode three different dressage tests that day in a 40x20 metre arena and even though I could not do much of an extended trot with this huge horse in such a small arena or conform his neck to look like a dressage horse, his geometry and rhythm were perfect and each time I had to do a 10- metre circle I would just start laughing again. Major will remain one of the greatest horses I have ever ridden with a heart bigger than himself.

Another Major success for both horse and rider! *California*

Between the tests, my fellow competitors would tell me that at least I had not wasted a trip to California; at least I got to compete, even if it was on a *draft horse*, and they also insinuated that I would never get the required scores to qualify for the Paralympic Selection Trials.

45

At the end of the day, when all the scores were posted, I got three Paralympic qualifying scores and with the highest score of the day, I also received the High Point Award Ribbon.

Oh what a glorious day that was and a fabulous reminder to *"Never Look a Draft Horse in the Mouth!"*

Horses Saved my Coffee Cups

Horses saved my coffee cups! When I say that to people, they make a polite comment to me then turn to the person sitting next to them and say, "What is she talking about?" So, let me share this story with you.

Riding horses at Equest totally changed my life for the better. One of the things I learnt over time was to think about and do more than one thing at a time. I used to be very good at multi-tasking and since "My Opportunity," that has become an issue for me. While learning to ride horses at Equest, my coach Gail had to continually tell me to keep my heels down, keep my back straight and upright and look in the direction I wanted the horse to go. This was a challenge for me - I would get my heels down and then slump over in my spine or look in the direction I wanted to go and totally forget about my feet.

I would also get feedback from the horses I was riding if I did not combine all these commands at the same time. By feedback I mean, if I was not giving them the correct cues, I did not get the outcome I wanted. For example, if my heels were down correctly and I wanted the horse to slow down and go right and yet I was looking left and leaning forward, I would not get my desired outcome. Over time and with Gail's patience, I started to multi-task on the back of the horse.

After many, many months of riding, my family and friends noticed that all these reminders, continuous reinforcement and lessons learnt from being in the saddle were transferring to my day-to-day living and allowing me to multi-task at home once again!

So, in the early years of "My Opportunity," if I was holding a cup of coffee in my right hand and the phone would ring or someone knocked on the door, I would drop the cup to pick up the phone or drop the coffee cup to wheel myself over to answer the door. Over time, the re-enforcement from Gail and the feedback received by these amazing horses, allowed me to multi-task once again. Now, I can put down the coffee cup and *then* pick up the phone or wheel myself over to the door. So, *horses saved my coffee cups!*

Over the years, I have had many people tell me that I should have just used plastic mugs to solve that problem. If I had done that, I would not have made these amazing changes in my brain, which has allowed me to grow, change and multi-task once again. Yes, *one brain injury will change your mind.*

It continues to amaze and delight me, how an hour in the saddle once a week can have such a positive effect on my day-to-day living. Even though I am the one in the saddle, the benefits I receive are experienced and enjoyed by all my family and friends. I now have an unbridled enthusiasm and a passion for living thanks to all the horses (and humans) that gave me a new lease of life.

Patience and Flexibility

Prior to "My Opportunity" I had a lot of patience and flexibility. Perhaps, one of the ways I demonstrated those characteristics was by being so independent and having the ability to drive myself around and make my own decisions. This afforded me the luxury of being patient and flexible. After "My Opportunity" I lost my ability to cope and enjoy these virtues.

I have learnt over time, that the person with the most patience and flexibility wins! I had to face my deficiencies in these two precious areas of my life, and when I did, I was able to seek out new and different ways to cultivate and use these tools again.

Due to the physical injuries I sustained and my impaired vision, I was no longer afforded the privilege of driving. The real reason here is that I do not have any friends with enough of a sense of humour or enough insurance to let me drive their cars!

Not being able to drive is still a major void in my life. It was an emotional roller coaster for me to have to rely on friends and family to take and fetch me or to wait for the bus from the outpatient therapy centre to transport me.

Not long before "My Opportunity," the Dallas Area Rapid Transport system (DART) introduced a public transportation service available to people with disabilities who were unable to use their regular bus and train systems. These included wheelchair-accessible mini-vans referred to as ParaTransit vehicles.

After "My Opportunity," I applied for this service. Once I was interviewed and certified as a ParaTransit rider, I was issued a DART ID card which afforded me the right to use this ParaTransit system. Reservations for this curb-to-curb shared-ride transportation service, called handi-rides, were made by calling into their office and requesting a ride to therapy, a doctor's appointment and even to the local supermarket or mall.

This service offered a sense of freedom and independence for me and yet the downside was that the reservations for handi-rides could only be made three days prior to the required date and they booked up very quickly. This resulted in not always being able to get a ride to my scheduled appointments or if I could get a ride on that particular day, it could involve many hours of waiting, sometimes getting picked up more than three hours before I needed to be at my appointment and then waiting for many hours after I was done, before my scheduled return ride would arrive to take me home.

So, as much as I appreciated the efforts by the City to help citizens like myself gain back some sort of independence, it was very hard on my body and so frustrating for my mind, to just sit in my wheelchair and wait for hours and hours and hours.

In the beginning of this DART experience, I would get really anxious and upset if the handi-ride did not arrive within its 20 minute pick up time window because it was running really late or if it did not pick me up at all due to mechanical failure or personnel issues, etc. This anxious behaviour I was experiencing was becoming detrimental to me and moving me further away from my goal of gaining back some sense of independence and freedom.

Once I realized this, I started to change my thoughts about it and in turn my behaviour changed too. I was practicing the art of patience and learning to be more flexible in my behaviours. I started to enjoy this time and made a conscious decision to use this time to my advantage by watching the squirrels and listening to the birds or speaking with others while I was waiting. Sometimes, I would listen to motivational tapes and use the time constructively instead of filling my mind and body with stress and anxiety levels that would take down even the strongest and biggest person.

It is interesting to note an analogy here. If you have some money and you waste it, then you are out of money for that moment and you can replace it; yet if you have wasted time, then you are out part of your life that can never be replaced. Money can come and go and yet we can never recapture yesterday, this morning or even an hour ago. Waste an hour of your precious day and you have wasted 60 golden minutes of your life.

I continue to use the wonderful services of DART and I am grateful for the surrounding cities that support this system. Now I enjoy my time out of the house and I have met the most amazing people whose paths I would not have crossed, if not for sitting somewhere in my wheelchair, just-a-waiting for my handi-ride!

Patience and flexibility – two wonderful tools that I continue to use every day! Now that's a handi-ride on my journey through life!

**Rain, sleet or snow –
we continue to ride in the Paralympic Trials.
Festival of Champions. *New Jersey***

Neuro-Linguistic Programming

Neuro-Linguistic Programming, NLP, is a model for understanding and duplicating excellence in human behaviour through the art of communication and behavioural change technology. It is built around the model that the human brain is a biological computer and, like all computers, it needs a software package that enables it to operate.

The software that runs our brain is our linguistic package. These are the words that we use in communicating with others and the thoughts we have in communicating with ourselves. NLP in its simplest terms states that the way we communicate, how we put together our communications, will do more to affect our outcomes than any other single factor. If we change how we think, we will change our reality. NLP can be likened to a user's operation manual for the brain.

About a decade before "My Opportunity," I had the distinct pleasure and good fortune of meeting and studying with my mentor and now good friend Jan, founder of NLP Learning systems in Dallas. Jan is a wise and wonderful woman who is about 20 years ahead of her time with her information, knowledge and insight. Over time, I took all of the NLP trainings, culminating in becoming a Master NLP practitioner. I am blessed to know Jan and so fortunate to have the incredible tools of NLP under my belt to access any time I need help - in fact, I use them every day to manage my life.

Before "My Opportunity," I had studied and taught NLP for over seven years and so many of the tools I needed and exercises used to achieve certain outcomes were well embedded in my brain.

I accessed these tools every day, several times a day. Most of this was now being done automatically without me having to think about each step along the way.

After "My Opportunity," I still remembered *some* of my NLP training and could access some of the tools I needed. Often times I would know what outcome I wanted and yet I had forgotten the process or exercise needed to get me there. The opposite of this was also true for me. To this day, I continually have to read and re-remember and re-learn many of the NLP techniques.

After "My Opportunity," I was like a newborn. I had to relearn so many things and start my life again from the beginning, even though I was already in my mid 30's. I started by using the effects of linguistics on my healing and recovery process. What I mean by this, is the use of language as a tool for healing.

For example, I would refer to my left leg as the less strong leg, still implying that it was strong, instead of saying, the weak one or the paralyzed one. It was always fascinating to me, how so many of my therapists would use words like weak or non-working when referring to my left leg. They were unconsciously reinforcing the negative without being aware of their behaviours and how these words were having an impact on the minds of their patients. Of course, I chose to let them know what I was thinking and asked that they refer to those parts of my body in a more positive way. Most of them were appreciative of this information and started using it with me on a regular basis as well as with their other patients.

Another way I used language in my healing process was incorporating the word "yet" into my thinking and spoken words. If there was a task or a behaviour I was unable to do, I would say that I am unable to do it YET... demonstrating my expectation to accomplish it in the future.

I would also use positive words to describe how I was feeling, even if I was down and hurting. I would say that every day in every way I was better, better and better. Really, who wants to hear your troubles and your woes day in and day out? Also, I did not want to re-affirm and reinforce any negative thoughts in my brain, ultimately perpetuating the same negative state rather than improving things!

The continued use of positive reinforcement and the use of positive words, created a positive environment and a positive route in my brain. I have always believed that we are what we think and even though this brain injury did *change my mind*, I still make it my mission to use positive linguistics and think positive thoughts through conscious choice. Over time, they have and they will continue to be embedded in my conscious mind and in that part of my brain that operates below the level of conscious awareness.

Another time comes to mind. Not long after "My Opportunity" I was very bitter at my situation and really did not know how to get better at accepting my new life. I started writing out some of the issues in my life that I longed to be different and I made an amazing discovery for myself. I had written that I wanted to go from *bitter to better* and realized that all I had to do was change one vowel to make this happen! One vowel – changing the "i" from bitter into an "e" turned that word into better. Once I did that and continued to reinforce better in my life and in my thinking through conscious choices every day, I was an easier person to be around. I exuded a more positive attitude and everything around me changed. I experienced more positive people and enjoyed more positive experiences. This allowed me to move forward instead of keeping myself stuck!

I am truly blessed that most of my family and friends have studied NLP. This enables them to continue to reinforce positive statements and encourage positive behaviours and actions within me at all times!

What exactly does positive thinking mean? Perhaps you, like me, have heard that said many, many times... just think positive! Just thinking that we are thinking positive is not going to make anything happen. We need to know the process involved to make this happen. Become aware of your thoughts, then in turn become aware of the emotions that are triggered by those thoughts and then become fully conscious of how these affect your actions. It is about reprogramming your brain to deliver to you, the best life possible.

Initially this may seem strange to you, it did to me too. I was not aware of how much internal dialogue and negative self-talk I was doing inside my head when I was thinking. I was also unaware of the many pictures and visuals that were flashing though my mind all day. When I became aware of them, I could more easily change them. If you are not aware of something happening, how can you do anything to change it or make it different? If you are unaware that you smoked the last three cigarettes, or ate half of the cheese cake or swore like a sailor in front of strangers, it is nearly impossible to change the behaviour.

This is especially useful if something in your life is not working the way you want it to. If you always do the same behaviour, you will always get the same results. This is like watching the same movie over and over and expecting a different ending each time! Albert Einstein defined insanity as: "*doing the same thing over and over again and expecting a different result.*"

If something is working well for you, continue to think those same thoughts, feel those same emotions and you will continue to get the same desired results. If something is not working for you, change the thoughts associated with that, then your emotions will change, followed by a change in your actions resulting in a different outcome.

There are so many different facets of NLP that I use on a daily basis and I invite you to find out more information if you want to make any changes in your life by visiting: www.NLPLearningSystems.com

Tammy took me jet skiing in the Gulf of Mexico and the Atlantic Ocean from Key West. *Florida*

Goal Reaching

Jan, from NLP, also introduced me to goal reaching - not goal setting, *goal reaching*. As she says, "If your intention is just to set them, then call it goal setting. If your intention is to reach them, then call it goal reaching." This is another example of how linguistics influences our everyday life. I am a very goal oriented individual and the best part of reaching my goals, is who I am becoming in the process.

Here's how I do my goal reaching. During the first week of January, I get some foam core poster board and a bunch of old magazines, a pair of scissors and a glue stick. I then put on some of my favourite music and I start to thumb through the magazines. When a picture, phrase or word gets my attention, I cut them out from these magazines and put them in a pile. These represent some of my goals that *I will reach* during the course of the year.

Now it is important for me not to rationalize or justify each and every picture at this time - I just allow myself to daydream as I do this exercise. I have found that in the past, if I stop to work out the fine details of how I am going to reach that specific goal, I will sabotage it and allow my rational thinking to limit me in my outcomes.

After I have gone through all the magazines, I proceed to paste down all the cut out words and pictures onto the foam core board, my new *goal reaching* board for that year is now ready. When complete, I place it in my room where I will see it every day, several times a day. This reinforces those images and words in my mind, to enable me to reach my goals.

A few years ago, I put a picture of a motor home on my goal board. I had several people laugh at me, as they know that due to my impaired vision, I do not drive anymore, so they thought it funny that I should put a motor home on my goal reaching board. They were limited in their thoughts. Just because I did not drive, did not mean that a motor home could not be introduced into my life.

Well the joke was on them, when in the summer of that same year, I took a trip with Tammy in her 37-foot motor home. So, even though I do not drive and I do not own a motor home, my goal was reached and I get to take several trips a year and travel in this wonderful motor home with all our dogs.

When I place pictures on my goal reaching board, I eliminate the need to know the exact route needed to reach these goals and therefore I am not limiting myself to the specifics. I wanted a motor home in my life and I got it.

Here is another one of my many goals that I have reached, from doing this goal reaching exercise. It is important to note here that our goals may not always come in the exact shape, colour or size that we are initially reaching for and yet, more often than not, they are bigger and better than we could ever have imagined. Be flexible in this - times change, our lives change (trust me, that one I know!!!) and our priorities shift.

Before "My Opportunity," I had wanted to go skiing and over the years I had occasionally put that on my board. After "My Opportunity," I could not imagine ever getting the chance to go skiing, as I could barely sit up in my wheelchair by myself, let alone go down a snow covered mountain. Even though I knew that this thought was limiting me, I stopped placing that visual on my goal reaching board because I allowed myself to believe it impossible to reach.

A few years later, when I was physically stronger, I entertained the idea of skiing again and added it onto my goal reaching board. Not long after that, Helen told me of a place in Colorado that offered a similar programme to Equest with horse riding in the summer and skiing in the winter months. This non-profit organization called Challenge Aspen, used adaptive equipment to teach riding and skiing to adults and children with physical and mental disabilities.

I did not know how I was going to pay for such a trip and yet I did not allow myself to get caught up in those details - thinking I would cross that bridge when the chance to go skiing presented itself. For the next two years, I continued to put skiing pictures on my board as well as a picture of Challenge Aspen that I got off the internet. This is how the story unfolded for me to reach my skiing goal.

Steve, a talented editor, wrote this amazing two-page article entitled Miss Independence, that was published in the Dallas Morning News. It was about my family and me, Equest and the benefits of therapeutic horse riding. This article was seen one Sunday morning by Rosa, a woman from Aspen Colorado, who was involved in the making of a documentary movie called "From Fear to Faith - Ordinary People, ExtraOrdinary Lives." She just happened to be in Dallas that weekend when the article was published.

She searched for my telephone number and soon found out that my number was unlisted. She persisted and finally got through to my Dad on the phone. She spoke with him and he took a message. He called me immediately and I returned Rosa's phone call. It is interesting to note here that Dad was hard of hearing and did not often answer the telephone. When he did answer the phone, he very rarely got all the digits in the phone number written down correctly or even a name. Well this day, he got it all together! Thanks Dad.

After meeting with Rosa, one thing led to another and she invited me to be a part of this documentary film that she was co-producing. At first, they came to film me competing in the national

UPHA Exceptional Challenge Cup event in Kansas City, where I was riding a beautiful Arabian mare from Equest called Zena.

Then, Rosa asked me if I had skied before. I told her that I had never skied and in fact, had not seen much snow in my lifetime. At that point in our conversation, she invited Tammy and me to stay at her home in Aspen to go skiing as part of the documentary. *Interesting to note here that Tammy also had skiing on her goal reaching board!*

She continued to share with me that the documentary would include Dr. Deepak Chopra, Dr. Richard Moss, Father Thomas Keating and another woman who was a paraplegic and a skier. Her name was Amanda and she was one of the founders of … wait for it… Challenge Aspen! (One of the skiing pictures on my goal reaching board) wow!!

Rosa arranged our trip to Colorado and then filmed me while I learnt to ski down Snowmass Mountain, using adaptive ski equipment from Challenge Aspen. The actual skis were attached to a legless chair like contraption and I sat in this with my legs supported straight out in front of me. In my right hand I had a very miniature ski pole to guide myself and on the left side of the equipment, there was another rigid ski pole attached to the equipment. I was securely fastened into this "ski chair" and I was being guided by Thomas, this gorgeous instructor from South America. The super creative cameraman Tom, was snowboarding next to me as I skied down the mountains, gathering some amazing footage for the documentary film. It was my first time to ski and see that much snow and it was totally exhilarating, a pure rush of adrenalin and a party for all of my senses.

Now, even in my wildest dreams, I could never have imagined the course of events that unfolded, allowing me to reach my goal of skiing. Coincidence? I think not! The power of g*oal reaching*? I think so!

Here is another fun filled goal reaching event for me to share. Every year, I put driving on my goal board. Even though my eye sight is not yet at a point where I could pass the eye test to get my licence again, I know it will happen. Well after several years, I did in fact get to drive – I got to drive a horse and cart. I started taking lessons in cart driving at Equest and had the very best time.

Equest has a very special cart that is wheelchair accessible. My volunteers would roll my wheelchair up into the cart with the use of an attached ramp. Once in the cart, the ramp would fold up and attach itself to the back of the driving cart. Next to me was

Tammy and I are on the top of the world, skiing in Aspen. *Colorado*

seated my driving instructor, referred to as an AB whip – an able-bodied instructor, who also had a set of driving reins only to be used if my situation became unsafe. Attached in front of us was my amazing four-legged friend, a Norwegian Fjord named Alman, who was going to teach me a thing or two about horse and cart driving.

Sometimes our goals may appear in our lives in a way other than we had imagined and yet ultimately, we have reached our goal. I wanted to drive to be more independent and that is exactly what horse and cart driving did for me. *If you aim at nothing, you will certainly hit it….nothing!*

So, with all the information, tools and techniques I have learnt and continue to learn through the use of NLP, I continue to walk my talk, or in my case, *wheel my words!*

Deb, Jen and Alman - cart driving at Equest. *Texas*

From Independent
to Totally Dependent

Due to my injuries and specifically because of my impaired vision, I am unable to drive a motor vehicle, yet. My eyesight is such that I have no depth perception and everything appears flat and out of focus. My right eye sees movement and mostly light and dark with no specific definition. My left eye can do rather well to focus if I close my right eye and the object in view is in a fixed position with no movement. As soon as I have to move my eyes to track something, I see everything as a blur and sometimes as a double image, thus making driving a huge hazard and really not an option for me yet!

So, this is a temporary challenge that I am dealing with on a daily basis - a loss of freedom and independence and being totally dependent on others for transportation. I need to add at this point that even though I am the driver in my life's journey, I am the worst passenger in someone else's car. This is due to how I see and perceive the other cars and the traffic around us. It appears that everyone is so close and we are all using one large piece of road with cars coming and going in the same lanes. Although I am getting better at controlling my outbursts as to what I think is happening out there, this is always a huge leap of faith for me, to feel relaxed and at ease as a passenger.

My family and friends are mostly very patient with my comments and perceived observations, while they are transporting me around. In fact, some even give me gifts when I ride with them. Some years ago, my friends Gwapie Jen and her mom, MaMa Jo drove me from Dallas to St Louis, Missouri to compete in a

Paralympic Qualifying Dressage Competition. This is about a ten-hour drive in good weather.

Upon pulling out of my driveway at the start of this adventure, they gave me a gift, a pair of bright orange large rimmed sunglasses. *Sounds very thoughtful right?* I thought so too until I put on these glasses and realized that they had painted over the lenses with black paint so I could see nothing at all while wearing them. We had a good laugh and headed north to St. Louis to join Sandy at her barn for the competition. It rained the entire trip and I would have been a complete basket case, and probably sitting on the side of the highway after they would surely have dumped me, had it not been for my bright orange rimmed "see nothing, say nothing" glasses.

Yes, we are still great friends and due to the freezing rain and below zero temperatures we experienced, we fondly refer to this road trip as our week in the state of misery, (Missouri).

We had so much fun on that trip that MaMa Jo left her home near Houston, Texas and came to stay with me in my Richardson house for about six weeks to help me out. I continued to wear those orange glasses when she drove me around in her "caddy" that zigged and zagged through traffic. However, they did nothing for me when we would round a corner and MaMa Jo would hit the curb. Needless to say, we would refer to MaMa Jo's car, as "Curby."

Even though I am still dependent on a lot of people for a lot of things in my life, especially transportation, I feel a lot more independent in my mind and in my attitude. I have turned the fear of being dependent into yet another opportunity to explore and experience.

Spontaneous

The dictionary meaning of this word includes the following: *a natural impulse or tendency; without effort or premeditation; natural and unconstrained; unplanned: acting upon sudden impulses.*

It was a hard transition for me, going from being an independent able-bodied woman with the choice of being spontaneous to becoming totally dependent and having everything planned for me. My bathing routine was carefully planned and scheduled. My meals were planned, as were the time schedules for my family and friends to be with me or to take me to my medical appointments or therapy sessions.

Now that I am in a wheelchair and not driving myself around or jumping into the shower or dashing off on a moment's notice to see a concert or have dinner with friends, it would appear that spontaneity was not happening in my world *yet*.

I like to think of spontaneity as a matter of perspective. I can still be spontaneous, it just take hours instead of minutes to get ready. My friends and family are really patient with me as we "plan" to be spontaneous. After I adjusted to this planned spontaneity, it was exciting to think that down the road, as I became stronger and more independent, I would not have to have everything so planned out for me anymore and I could truly become more spontaneous more quickly!

The one thing that was truly spontaneous about my life then, was the calling of my bladder. This reminds me of one time when Helen and I were eating dinner at a local restaurant in Richardson and suddenly I needed to use the loo (restroom). Helen asked the waiter as to the location of the restroom and we were pointed to a door facing the tables and directly opposite the entrance. Helen wheeled me over there and pushed open the door expecting to find a larger room with a toilet and a sink. To our surprise, the door opened inward, directly to the toilet. We attempted to get me into the loo but my wheelchair prevented the door from closing, so we attempted to transfer me out of my chair onto the toilet seat and this did not work either. This loo, just like my bladder, had very limited space! I had to go and I had to go right then! Helen, who is such a creative thinker, gathered up a few artificial plants and trees from around this small restaurant and stacked them in front of the open restroom door. She then enlisted the assistance of some of the employees and lined them up shoulder to shoulder, facing outwards of course, in front of the plants, thereby creating a shield between me and the other patrons. What a relief!

We dined out on this story for a very long time. That restaurant closed not too long after our one and only visit - it certainly would not have met the Americans with Disabilities Act (ADA) requirements that we have in place today.

Oh my wordy, here is another bladder story that is so funny. Tammy and I went to a wonderful French bakery for dinner one evening. We were seated outside on the patio enjoying our meal, when I needed to go, go, go!

I found the loo and proceeded to enter the handicap stall. I was in the process of transferring across to the toilet seat when I heard this very crisp and clear man's voice, asking, "Are you American!"

I got such a fright that I pulled myself up and almost went headfirst into my awaiting wheelchair. This statement was almost immediately followed by another man's voice saying something in French.

It was only then that I realized that these voices were coming from a recorded message, an entertainment idea in the restroom whereby one sentence was in English followed by a sentence in French.

I finished up and headed back onto the patio to resume my dinner. Tammy asked me if everything was all right as I had tears rolling down my face. She soon realized that these tears were being caused by my laughter, as I attempted to tell her what had just happened. I could only get one or two words out a time as I was laughing uncontrollably by now. Even though Tammy did not get the full story for a very long time, she too was laughing so hard, not at me, just with me. Can you say oui, oui?

Finally we stopped laughing and finished our dinner. While having some yummy French desert and coffee, I remember looking up and thinking how bright and beautiful the full moon was shining down on us. I pointed this out to Tammy and told her it felt like it was close enough for me to touch it.

She asked where the full moon was and I was amazed that she was not seeing it. Again I pointed up to it and asked her how she could miss it. It was so bright and big and even I, with impaired vision could see it clearly. After many attempts of trying to see the full moon, Tammy got out of her chair and walked all around the table, looking up from the patio, to see this spectacular event and still nothing. I continued to describe it to her and was amazed that she still did not see it. Finally she got right behind me and had her eyes level with mine and turned her face in the same direction as mine as I again pointed to the moon.

At this point she laughed so loud it took her a few minutes to compose herself and inform me that it was not the full moon I was seeing – it was a street light shining through the trees. Oh my wordy…. There went my ability to spontaneously recognize things. What a fantastic evening of fun and laughter. Even with my impaired vision, we have found things to laugh at together. We can find humour in even the smallest event and laugh until tears roll down our faces. Laugh so much that we are unable to speak for several minutes. Laugh so much that our bellies hurt. Laugh so much that the coffee I just swallowed is now sprayed across the table and dripping out of my nose.

It is fascinating to me that so many able-bodied people, with no "disabilities or major challenges" in their lives, have a hard time finding anything to laugh at. Their negative mental attitude is more disabling for them than my physical condition is to me.

For me, a day without laughter is a wasted day. Laughter is healthy. Laughter is like taking an anti-anxiety prescription tablet – it can be addictive, yet has no negative side effects. So far, there are no scientific warnings against laughing.

One other funny spontaneous story, also bladder related, was on my first entry into the USA through JFK airport in New York City, when I was able-bodied. Before heading to get my backpack from the baggage claim, I stopped into the restrooms. After going to the toilet, I stood up to button up my jeans and suddenly the toilet flushed itself. I was so shocked that I let out a high-pitched scream and spun around to see who had gotten into this little cubicle with me to flush the toilet. When I realized it was an automatic flushing toilet, I laughed until I had tears rolling down my cheeks. That toilet was really high tech and quite foreign for me. This was my first introduction into the United States and I still chuckle over this scenario!

Get Creative

Being creative, for me, is using different resources to get "the job" done. An example of this is the way I open the little sugar packets in a restaurant – I hold the packet in my right hand and tear it open using my teeth. It may not look very attractive and yet the ultimate outcome is the same. I also use my teeth to hold my riding glove as I push my right hand into it, before I start my therapy riding lessons.

Most people would not consider these actions as "normal," and yet the only "normal" I know is found on the dial settings of a washing machine between super-wash and delicate!

MaMa Jo and Gwapie Jen got me back into the fun of fishing, by making me a holder for my fishing rod out of some rope and a piece of PVC pipe. They would tie this contraption around my waist and I could place the rod into the pipe when I needed to use my right hand to reel in a fish. This was an interesting sight to see and yet it worked. I would like to add here that when I caught a fish, I would make a kissing gesture to the fish and release it back into the water. Sometimes, with my lack of depth perception, my mouth and the fish would actually make contact. Fishing for me, is about the same as most teenage relationships, *catch and release.*

I continue to love fishing. I am truly blessed with amazing friends who love me more than their fishing rods. This is so evident when we are fishing and I catch a fish, lose my bait, or get my hook stuck on something far down in the murky waters. It takes one of my friends, Tammy, Skipper, Nano, Marty or Sue, to stop what they are doing to help me get myself back on track so I can continue to fish again. This is a huge gift of friendship – giving up their opportunity to catch a fish to help me.

Some time ago, I went salmon fishing in Alaska, with Tammy, Mom Billie and Dad Wendell. We were on an Alaskan cruise with nine other family members and friends and yet we were the only four that chose to go on this half-day deep sea fishing excursion.

When I was making reservations for this side trip, I was told numerous times that many of the captains would not take me on their fishing boats because of my wheelchair and also that I would not manage to pull in the salmon with the use of only one hand – it's a good thing that not one of us believed that, including our captain and deck hand on this fishing boat.

We took off in the fishing boat to catch some bait then it was off into the deep sea to start our adventure. The others on the boat caught themselves some huge salmon and I was busy *wishing me a fish.* Sure enough, my turn came and it was time to get creative – nothing had been planned or practiced for this event, it just happened. I had a bite and definitely had a huge salmon at the end of my line. Now, how do I pull this fish into the boat with only one hand?

Immediately, Dad Wendell got behind me and put his arms around my waist to act as an anchor for me to ensure that I did not go swimming with the salmon. Mom Billie held the fishing rod against my belly for support and Tammy would help me reel in my catch while the deck hand got in front of me and balanced my fishing rod on his shoulder. The deck hand would bend down and forward which would lower the fishing rod and Tammy and I would reel in like crazy, then he would stand up, which put pressure on the line, making it taut.

This unpracticed dance of friends went on for a very long time until finally we landed this huge salmon in our fishing boat. We were all exhausted and I was totally amazed at how our little village came together to catch this salmon. Totally unrehearsed, it just worked out great. *The gift of creativity among friends.*

We caught many salmon that day and had them frozen and sent back to Dallas to enjoy with all our family and friends. We also had a large salmon taken back to the ship where one of the chefs prepared it fresh for our group of thirteen to enjoy for dinner that night.

The moral of the story here is: *never underestimate the power of creativity!*

(l-r) Mom Billie, Tammy, Dad Wendell and I with our awesome catch of 37 salmon. *Alaska*

(Before "My Opportunity")
I am having fun in a pay phone booth in London
– they really did exist! *England*

I Can See Enough
to Laugh at Myself

With everything I have been through, I am very blessed to have always maintained my sense of humour.

For a long time, my family, friends and even my neighbours had the daily ritual of walking my dogs Kei and Sagie. Now, the time had come for me to explore the adventure of "walkies." I was unable to hold two leashes and wheel my manual wheelchair with just my right hand, so I got creative and attached their leashes to either side of my wheelchair so we could go for walks. This worked well for all of us until one afternoon, while going "walkies" in the neighbourhood, Sagie saw a squirrel on the right side of the street and Kei saw a bunny in the bushes to the left side.

Going "walkies" with Kei and Sagie. *Texas*

It was amazing that they both decided to make a dash for these little critters at exactly the same time, and suddenly, I became a human slingshot. I was catapulted out of my chair like a pebble from a slingshot, landing in a neighbour's flowerbed. It was a soft-landing and I was laughing so much that I could hardly lift my head up from between the flowers!

The dogs continued to chase their critters, battling back and forth for leadership as to who could pull my chair the furthest, and in which direction! As my wheelchair was being bounced down the street, it made a lot of noise, which in turn made Kei and Sagie run faster and wilder than before! With all this barking and noise, some neighbours came out to help. The look on their faces turned from utter distress and panic to laughter when they knew I was ok. My laughter was coming from deep in my belly and is so contagious, that they had to join in on it.

Finally, they managed to catch my dogs and lift me back into my wheelchair. My chair now has many scratches and dents on it, always reminding me of this funny time. One of the neighbours followed us back home and everything turned out just wonderful. Dogs + Laughter = Healing.

It is very ok to laugh at yourself. I do it a lot and it has helped in the healing process. Really when you think about it, this could have been an experience that had a negative impact on me for the rest of my life. Instead I turned it around and I continue to use that image of me in the flower bed and my two dogs dragging my empty wheelchair down the street, to make myself laugh out loud.

It is well known and stated often, that laughter is the best medicine as it has so many positive benefits on the body. Laughter can be contagious and infectious. It can bring people together and often breaks the ice in a tense situation. Laughter helps shift perspective and can often lighten our load. I encourage you to seek out opportunities in your life that make you laugh and never underestimate the power of a good belly laugh!

Kei and Sagie are now playing at the Rainbow Bridge.
Heaven

Doctor Norman Cousins, in his book *Anatomy of an Illness*, emphasizes the benefits of laughter to heal the body. Dr. Cousins was able to get some pain relief when he started using positive emotions to produce positive chemical changes in his body, proving that the mind is an effective healing tool. He cites many studies that have been conducted, to prove the potency of laughter and humour as a means to improve health and reduce pain.

I practiced on yet another borrowed horse, to qualify for the Paralympic Trials. *New York*

I feel like Royalty with this Prince. *Texas*

Choices - Respond or React

After "My Opportunity," I had the choice of just lying around and allowing everyone to plan out all my daily routines and tell me how my life would be, or I could choose to take an active part in these decisions. I could have chosen to become just a passenger in my new life, or I could get into the driver's seat. I chose to be the driver and not the passenger through my life's journey. Are you the driver or passenger in your life? You can choose to make things happen or you can just standby and wonder, what happened!

We are always in a position to make choices in our lives. The question is; are you willing to make choices that might be difficult, yet will benefit you in the long run or will you choose to make choices that are not going to serve you well in the long haul because it seems easier right now? Granted, sometimes the choices may not appear to be between two positive idealistic situations and yet, there are still choices to be made. The reality is that we are never sure exactly how things are going to unravel and mostly we are delighted with the outcomes. Outcomes that we probably could not have even imagined possible!

Imagine arriving at a fork in the road - we can choose to just stay stuck at the fork or make the choice and go down one of the roads. We do not always know where the road may lead and yet we always get to choose the way we respond to the situation and our environment. How we respond to the choices before us and the choices that we make, is what makes the difference. If we look at everything and feel that it is a negative situation and people around us tell us it is a negative situation, we will continue to perpetuate the negative. And yet, if we practice the art of looking for, and seeing the positive in everything and feeling positive about our choices, we WILL encourage and start to notice all the wonderful and positive events in our life. Like attracts like!

We cannot always control our external environment and yet we can always control how we respond to it - we can control how we choose to feel about it and what we do about it. For example, I could not control the driver of the vehicle that broadsided me back in 1996, and yet I can control how I handle the outcome of that incident. I could choose to look at all the doors that have slammed shut in my face and focus on all the losses I have encountered due to that, or I can (and I do) look for new doors and windows opening for me and venture out into a new day, every day focusing on what works best for me.

For me, one barn door opened and I galloped through it. These choices led me into an exciting new world filled with amazing horses and wonderful spiritual beings.

Each day is going to come and each day is going to go and we can never get yesterday back - so make a choice how to spend today - enjoy it and access the wonderful memories or lose it for all times! I have found it better for me to respond, rather than to react.

I know also, that everything we do, every decision we make, starts as a thought, and then we have a choice. Again, it may appear that the choices are not always what we want, and yet we are at choice. We can choose to respond or we can choose to react to any given situation. There is no question that many times in my life I reacted to my situation instead of responding to it and this did not work out well for me.

By choosing to respond to a given situation, I feel like I am more in control of my emotions and I am more responsible for my outcomes. Reacting to that same situation would leave me stuck and out of control, not a useful or healthy place to be.

I choose to look for and find the good in every situation - there is good in my situation too. I know that everything happens for a reason and even though I did not see the reasons or positive outcomes immediately, they were often revealed to me, years down the road, and are still being revealed to me, even now! Based on my history, I know that positive outcomes will continue to be revealed to me, so now I watch for them with anticipation and delight.

This is not to say that I stay in a positive frame of mind 24/7. I am human and I have my good hours and my not so good hours and yet the more I concentrate on the positive and the more I practice the things that are working for me, the better I become. I have learnt that if I want to change any given situation I have to change my thoughts about that situation first, which in turn changes my behaviours and this helps me to change my actions. I know that if something is not working for me and I continue to do the same behaviour and have the same thoughts, I will continue to get the same results. *(This is the definition of insanity in a nutshell)* If there is something that is working for me then I would repeat those thoughts, behaviours and actions to achieve those same great results again. Be at choice and respond as opposed to being mentally paralyzed and reacting – it is definitely kinder to your soul and healthier for your body.

I have met some people over the years that are more paralyzed in their mind than I am in my physical body. People who are literally paralyzed with fear! Mental paralysis can be equally as challenging as physical paralysis. If you are afraid to make a choice or just refuse to make choices in your life, your emotions can and will paralyze your mind. Take responsibility, make your life choices and respond to whatever shows up. Release your self-created mental paralysis, because YOU CAN!

This is a great story about responding or reacting: I was at the checkout counter at a local super store, when this lady walked up to me and bent down over my wheelchair and said, "I know exactly what you are going through in that wheelchair!" At first I was startled to see a stranger's face so close to my own face and then my next thought was, *you do not even know me, so how do you know what I am going through being in this wheelchair?*

As she lifted her left foot and pointed to her big toe, she continued to tell me that last summer, she had an ingrown toenail and for several days, the pain was so excruciating, she wondered if she would ever get through it. "The pain passed and look at me now, so hang in there sugar and everything will be alright!" she said as she patted me gently on my shoulder. Then she turned and walked towards the exit of the store.

The cashier and the people surrounding me at the time were just standing there with their jaws dropped open, in complete silence not sure what they should be doing at that exact moment. Then I loudly said to this complete stranger, "THANK YOU for your kindness and support."

I could have gotten upset and had a negative reaction, telling her that she knows nothing about how I feel, and yet instead, I decided to respond with a smile and thank her. This put all the people around me at ease and then they too started to comment on her kindness.

I came from a place of choosing to respond to her intention - not to what she said, but rather how she said, what she said. She came from a place of caring and concern and I chose to take it like that too. People do things for their own reasons, not yours and it is about how you respond or react to that, which will make all the difference.

You can choose to define yourself by what has happened to you or you can choose to define yourself by how you respond to what has happened to you.

Another time, I was in Houston visiting Skipper in hospital, after her heart surgery. Nan parked her truck and we made our way down this very long steep inside corridor to reach the lifts (elevators), to get to the ICU. Nano was walking and talking and I was free-wheeling next to her. There were not too many people in this corridor so I thought I would have a little fun with her and break the tension and anxiety that we were both feeling over our dear friend.

As Nan continued to talk, I allowed myself to wheel faster and faster down this corridor, then, I looked back at her and shouted, "Runaway wheelchair, runaway wheelchair." She was totally shocked by my behaviour as were the few other people in the corridor. She knew she had the power to choose between responding or reacting to my behavior.

Some of the people made exaggerated efforts to get out of my way and some just pointed and joined in on the joke when they saw I was actually in full control of my chair. This one lady flattened herself up against the wall in the hopes of not being seen by me – she just had no idea if she should react or respond to me in this situation, or just attempt to dissolve into the wall. She really had no clue as to how to handle this situation. At that moment, she was more paralyzed than I was.

Nano was way behind me and yet I could hear her response of laughter and telling me to stop, all the way down to the end of the corridor, where I was waiting for her. We were both laughing so much that we had to wait several minutes before entering the lift (elevator) to go up to the ICU to see our Skipper.

That was just what the doctor ordered, a great big serving of laughter.

Remember, you always have choices - Respond or React.

83

**Zena taught me about the extended trot.
Practicing for Team USA.** *Texas*

Fowl-Play

Then there was this time when I was checking out of a grocery store and my cell phone rang. I answered the call and agreed to a "drive-buy" at KFC with my friend Gwapie Jen. I hung up the phone and paid for my groceries.

While I was wheeling away from the counter, this very elegantly dressed lady who was behind me in the checkout line, followed me and tapped me on the shoulder. She said, "I could not help but overhear your private conversation and I want to tell you that my place of worship offers free counselling for people like you - people that are very angry and mad at life, after all, you are disabled and in a wheelchair!"

I must have looked very confused because I was very confused by what she was saying. She continued to preach to me that it was not necessary to arrange any drive-by shootings just because I could not cope with my life. She could help me.

Then the penny dropped and I understood how she had interpreted my not-so-private phone call. I started to smile and then laugh out loud. Now she had this very concerned and confused look on her face.

I thanked her for her kindness and explained that I was coping very well in my life. I also felt it necessary at this point to explain the drive-buy conversation. I had just made lunch arrangements with Gwapie Jen to pick me up at home, she would then **drive** us to Kentucky Fried Chicken and I would **buy** us the meal. Hence, a drive-buy!

She smiled politely, turned around and went back to pay for her groceries. There was no *fowl-play* here!

**Always having FUN. Deb & Tammy have (h)attitude –
where's my hat?** *Texas*

Focus

Focus on what you want - if you spend all your time focusing on what you have lost, on the doors that have closed in your life, then you will have spent your time doing just that – focusing on closed doors and being stuck just looking at all that you no longer have. It is impossible to see the new doors that have opened for you, when you are staring only at those that have slammed shut.

What you focus on, you will invite into your life. Imagine where I would be if I had stayed focused on all the doors that had slammed shut for me after "My Opportunity," instead of focusing on all the doors and windows that were and are opening up for me daily.

I will give you an example of everyday life and how things appear in our world when we focus on them. When my nephew and niece, Craig and Misty were expecting their son Preston, it was as if suddenly the entire City was pregnant. Every day, I would see a pregnant lady or hear about a friend or their family member that discovered they were pregnant. Due to the fact that I was thinking so much about this positive event in my life and I was more consciously aware of these thoughts, the news and appearances of more pregnant ladies was prominent for me. Pregnant ladies were always around, and yet it was only now that I was noticing them more than ever before, as this was my new centre of focus. Craig and Misty are now the proud parents of four fabulous sons.

(l-r) Cohen, Craig, Misty, Preston and twins Dawson and Dylan. *Texas*

The same can be said about purchasing a new car. You may not remember seeing a lot of them while driving around and now, suddenly you pull up next to one at every other robot (traffic light). Those cars had always been there, it is just that you had not noticed them until your focus was on this particular car.

Now taking those two everyday examples into account, does it make more sense to focus on the things you want in your life, rather than focusing on the things you don't want, or worse, focusing on nothing?

Have you ever noticed how many people know more about what they do not want in their lives versus what they do want? How many times have you and some friends decided to go out to dinner, and you may ask, "What are you hungry for?" Their replies are, "I do not want steak" or "I know I do not want pasta tonight" or "For sure I do not want to travel too far to that restaurant." These replies are all about what they do not want, and yet they cannot think of what they do want.

So many people run their lives like that - knowing what they do not want and yet they do not express and mostly, do not know what they do want. These people are inexplicably surprised when they continue to get what they do not want. Where is their focus?

We create our own reality - the universe will bring into our lives that which we think about. Our thoughts are like requests to the *Dear Universe Column* in the newspaper of life. Focus on and state more of what you want and move away from all that you do not want. The more you do this kind of thinking, the more you will get what you want and then it will become a habit - a great habit and a more positive force in your life.

Your subconscious mind is on a mission to make you right. If you believe that life is terrible and hard, your subconscious mind will make sure you are right by attracting things into your life that are terrible and hard. The converse is equally true. If you choose to focus on and believe that the universe is a friendly place, your subconscious mind will also go to work to ensure you are right. Either way, your subconscious is going to make you right, now the question is…what kind of a world do you want to be right in?

If you are one of those people who focus on what you do not want in your life, then this is a great exercise to help you focus on what you do want in your life. Get a piece of paper and draw a line down the centre. On the left side of the page, write down all the things you do not want in your life. Then go back and write the complete opposite of those on the right hand side of the page. It will be amazing to most people how quickly they can complete the left *don't want* side of the page and how much difficulty they have with the right, *I want* side of the page.

Here is an example of this: On the left side of the page, I may write, "I always get stuck in traffic on the way home!" The opposite of that statement for me is, "I enjoy steady moving traffic creating a clear and easy trip home."

Ensure that the opposite of what you want is stated in a positive way - avoid adding the word "not" to the same sentence!

For example, I always get stuck in traffic on the way home - I do *not* want to get stuck in traffic on the way home. Using the word "not" will still conjure up the same picture in your brain, of you being stuck in traffic, then your mind has to negate that picture to accommodate your language and for you to get your outcome. Well, as there are no pictures in our brains of "not" we are therefore still focusing on getting stuck in traffic!

A better way to state this would be, I enjoy steady moving traffic creating a clear and easy trip home. This conjures up a picture of a clear and easy trip home, and as you continue to visualize and focus on this, you will notice that this is more of what you will get in your life. After all, you are now focusing on exactly what you want.

If you are against war, you avoid anti-war rallies and attend peace rallies. Do not slam the door … close the door gently. (Aah that works). Do not fall out of the saddle… Stay safe and secure in your saddle. These are clearly the opposite situations, no ambiguity in this process – just clear, focused and simple requests to your brain.

Another example of this is getting good parking spots at the mall or shopping centres especially around the holidays. I always visualize and focus on getting a front row parking space wherever I go and most of the people I know tell me that I am just lucky. They continue to tell me that they have no luck and they always get stuck parking in the furthest spot in the entire parking lot. If that is what they think each and every time they go to the mall, then that is exactly what they will get. They have made a habit out of parking so far away from the entrance, that it has become a self-fulfilling prophecy for them, a self-perpetuating situation. Again, they focus on the furthest parking places, and that is exactly what they will get.

I often joke with my friends, that the main reason they take me shopping with them is to use my handicap-parking placard! In all reality, we usually park closer to the store entrance, in a regular parking space, because I focus on close-up parking. Even though I have a handicap-parking permit, these handicap accessible parking spots are very popular and often quite far away from the entrance to the stores.

So start to *focus* on what you want and continue to be amazed as it all comes into focus for you.

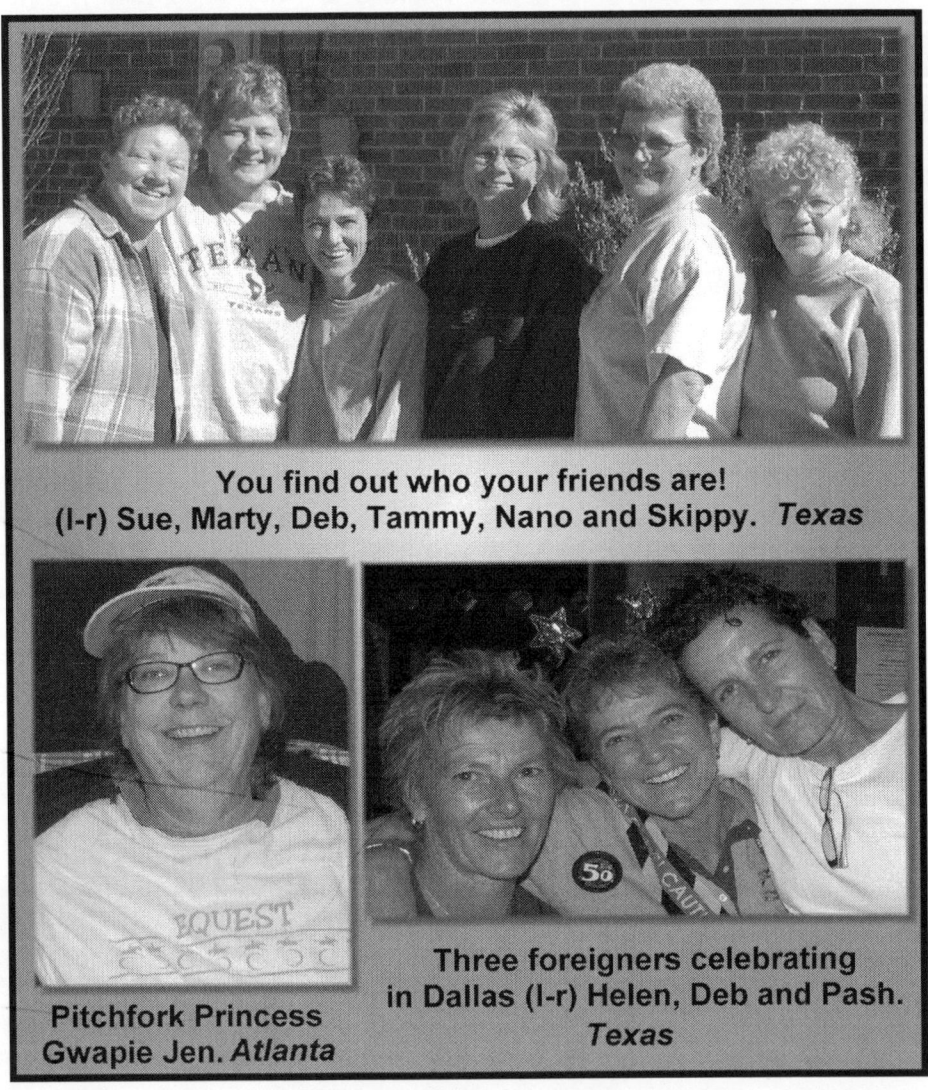

You find out who your friends are!
(l-r) Sue, Marty, Deb, Tammy, Nano and Skippy. *Texas*

Pitchfork Princess
Gwapie Jen. *Atlanta*

Three foreigners celebrating
in Dallas (l-r) Helen, Deb and Pash.
Texas

Giving and Receiving Assistance

This is still one of the most challenging adaptations I have to make in my life since "My Opportunity." I was always an independent, self-sufficient, help-others kind-of-person. I could do it all; rarely needed any help with anything except when I was playing in a team sport then it was a group effort for sure! I was the one who volunteered every spare hour I had to help those that needed help and now, I am that person that needs the help.

In retrospect, that part of my life was off balance - I rarely took time out for myself because I felt like I was receiving all I needed from helping and giving to others, and yet, that turned out to be very one-sided. If giving is like removing water from a well, there has to be a replenishing of water in order for the giving to continue. That would be the ideal balance.

So here I was, needing assistance 24/7 in all aspects of my daily routine. The first thing to go in this situation was my pride. I had friends bathing and changing me, shaving my legs, cutting my toenails & fingernails and taking me to the bathroom. Until now I had been a very private person. Even back in my younger years, I would wait for most of my fellow athletes to leave the sport facility locker rooms so I could shower and change in relative privacy.

What I have learnt over the years, is that most people are more than willing to assist me if they can and to my delight, they can say no if they are unable to do it. This honesty makes it a little easier for me to request and to accept assistance. I know how much I enjoyed being able to do for others and so perhaps this is a win-win situation. I am getting better at requesting assistance and I am working on the accepting and receiving part of this perfectly balanced equation!

This is a great story - I was at the Equest barn one morning, getting ready for my therapy-riding lesson. I was wheeling myself towards the door to enter the office area, when another rider, a young autistic girl, moved in front of me and pushed open the door for me. Even though I had become good at swinging open the door and I did not need any assistance with this task, I accepted her kindness and thanked her. To my surprise, her response was "You are the one that is disabled and I can help you!" *Giving and receiving* - what a wonderful balance in the lessons of life!

When I first started riding at Equest, I needed a lot of assistance. I needed help getting my riding gloves, helmet and chaps on. I needed assistance with grooming and tacking to get my horse ready for my therapy lesson. I needed two side-walkers to help me balance in the saddle and keep my feet in the stirrups, as well as another volunteer to help walk my horse around on a lead rope. Of course I also needed help mounting and dismounting my horse.

It was so very hard to accept all this help having been so very independent prior to "My Opportunity." After about one year of riding, I found I was able to start volunteering at Equest myself. I was at a point in my life, that I was able to help other riders get ready as well as talk to many future riders, parents and families about the benefits of therapeutic horse riding.

Being a rider and accepting assistance, then being a volunteer and assisting others was the perfect balance for me. I love giving and helping so much and even though I am still learning the lesson of accepting help, I do understand that I am more in harmony with the balanced idea of giving and receiving.

Everyone is blessed when we can give from our heart in a spirited manner and receive with appreciation and gratitude! Allowing others to help me has been a major challenge since "My

Opportunity" and even though I am still learning this lesson, I feel sure that I would not have learnt it, had it not been thrust on me.

This is really a life lesson worth learning *before* you too, get thrust into a situation like "My Opportunity." I invite you to learn from my experience and get the full benefits of this perfect balance of *giving and receiving assistance*, without having to have your own personal life altering, mind changing situation occur.

**Deb receiving assistance from Tammy
to stand on a moving glacier. *Alaska***

**We all volunteer in our local communities.
(l-r) Mom Billie and Dad Wendell, Rob and Joy,
Mom, Joe, Cousin Stan, Tammy,
little Kathy, Kathleen and Deb.**
New York

Volunteering –
Can You Spare some Change?

I grew up in a household that did a lot of volunteering. My precious Mom was always out there doing for others and got me involved in volunteering from the time I could walk. What a great gift of being able to volunteer and make a change in someone's life by doing something for them – *Thank you Mom*.

As a little girl, I got to push people around in wheelchairs even though I was not yet tall enough to see over the chairs. I assisted in events at group homes for children and adults with disabilities and I was always helping my Mom prepare thousands of goodie packages to send away to our armed forces, fighting in the bush. When I was older, I helped out in nursing facilities, often playing the guitar and singing along with the delightful residents at the senior citizens centres. There were also many summers when we had children from the local orphanage come and stay with us. What an amazing opportunity and a lifetime gift my parents gave to us.

I also volunteered as a nurses' aid in the hospital during the war in Rhodesia and it was at this time that I knew that I wanted to become a Paramedic.

A few years after "My Opportunity," I underwent major back surgery. While recovering, I volunteered most of my time at non-profit organizations. I am so passionate about Equest and their amazing horses that most of my speaking engagements were about the positive changes I experienced while being around horses and the benefits of therapeutic horse riding.

I did a lot of events with Carter BloodCare. Having been a recipient of blood transfusions during my 16-hour back surgery, I had a lot to be grateful for. I used this time to share my *attitude for gratitude* with the blood donors at their annual gala events and when I volunteered at some smaller events, I would share my story and encourage people to give the life-saving gift of blood. Save a life – it could be your own!

I also enjoyed speaking at the Texas Lions Clubs. One year, there were over 150 children between the ages of seven and sixteen, each one with a physical or mental disability, enjoying a week-long summer camp in beautiful Kerrville, Texas. I was invited to be their guest speaker over the weekend, so Tammy and Mom Billie drove me almost 300 miles from Dallas to Kerrville so I could share my experiences. I would speak and share stories with the children during the day and then in the evening, I would speak with the board members and adult volunteers about overcoming adversity and the amazing benefits of therapeutic horse riding.

During my interaction with the children, I gave out post-card sized photos of me on my white Equest horse and little gold medals to each and every child. I wanted these gifts to be a reminder of a positive and fun time and to encourage them to do their very best, each and every day.

Well, later that same summer, I was in a parking lot with my friend Dr. Pam. We were removing my power wheelchair from the back of her SUV when this gentleman came over and offered us some assistance. He mentioned that his daughter was in a wheelchair so he had a lot of wheelchair experience.

Of course, one of the first questions out of my mouth was had she ever been horse riding? He mentioned that earlier that summer, his daughter had attended a camp in Kerrville where she got to ride horses. He continued to tell me about this guest speaker at this camp who was paralyzed and in a wheelchair and she was now competing in horse riding events. He said that his daughter had a picture of this lady on a white horse by her bedside together with a gold medal. He told me that his daughter looked at this picture every day and even if she was having a rough day, she would be encouraged by this post-card sized picture, and say, "If she can do it, so can I."

As he was telling me this story in great depth, I noticed that he was getting closer and closer to my face. I wasn't sure if he was going to kiss me or what! Then suddenly he pulled back and exclaimed in a really loud voice, "It's you – it is you on that white horse. It is your picture and your story that encourages my daughter each and every day!"

I just burst into tears and then this stranger and I hugged for what seemed like a very long time. These were tears of joy and encouragement. I got to realize that my story and post-card picture of myself riding Zena had made such a positive impact on one little girl and her daddy. My ability and willingness to volunteer had changed their lives for all times.

Often times, we do not realize the impact each and every one of us can have in this life-time, just by what we say and what we do. I know that volunteering is the one action that gives you a higher return than your initial investment.

Give me a penny for my thoughts
and I will put in my two cents worth!

Remember to always taste your words
before spitting them out.

**How many siblings does it take to get my chair and I
down the stairs in a New York Subway,
when there is no working lift (elevator)?
Thanks Rob.** *New York*

Wheelchair Etiquette

I have noticed an interesting behaviour over the years, that most people assume that if you are in a wheelchair, you are totally incompetent and especially hard of hearing. Many times I have gone into a store, I ask the question and the sales person answers the able-bodied person standing next to me.

One day, Gwapie Jen and I went into a very large, well known do-it-yourself hardware store. I asked the salesman a question and he looked directly at Gwapie Jen and answered my question. I asked the question for the second time and again the same response and behaviour from the salesman. Then Gwapie Jen said, "Look, I am not a ventriloquist and you did not see my mouth move to ask the question." Pointing at me she said, "She asked the question, so answer her!"

At this point the salesman gets down on one knee to look at me eye-to-eye. Even though this was not a marriage proposal, I certainly appreciated him getting level with me. He then said in a very clear, slow paced and enunciated voice at a higher than normal volume, "Hello, my name is Jack and you have a question about replacing the blade in a circular saw?" While he is slowly articulating his sentence, he is also making exaggerated movements with his hands describing a circular saw. Of course I could have gotten really upset by his actions and that would have spoilt my entire day or I could have burst into laughter or even responded in a foreign language just to see his reactions. I will leave my response to your imagination and just let you know that I did finally get my question answered!

May I suggest to you, that you ask a person if they need assistance before just assuming. If you saw an able-bodied person walking up a hill, would you automatically go up to them, grab a hold of their arm and walk them to the top of the hill? Well the same holds true for a wheelchair user - ask the person if they need or want some help before just grabbing the handles of their chair and taking off.

I had that happen to me at a local mall. I was moving around slowly, just window-shopping whilst waiting on my friend Tammy to return to this, our designated meeting place. The next thing this strange man took hold of the handles at the back of my wheelchair and pushed me up the slope into the store entrance. I had NO desire to go into that store but he assumed I did and I am sure that he thought he was doing the right thing in assisting me. Of course he was nowhere to be found when I turned around to explain some wheelchair etiquette to him!! As a wheelchair user, I consider the chair as an extension of my body and I am not comfortable with people just touching me without my permission.

Another time, Helen and I were in the local supermarket to do some shopping and I was waiting for her in the pet department. I was looking up at the top shelf at all the different bird feeders, comparing sizes and prices on these feeders. The next minute, this stranger stopped in front of my wheelchair. She reached up on her tiptoes to the top shelf, grabbed the biggest box up there and sat it on my lap. Then, as quickly as she appeared, she was gone. She did not say a word and I was in shock and speechless. All I could see was this huge cardboard box about two inches away from my face.

I started laughing so hard and had to just sit and wait there for Helen to return, as I could not wheel myself anywhere. When she came around the corner to see what I was laughing at, she said all she could see were my legs hanging off the wheelchair, this bright coloured huge cardboard box on my lap, a few fingers from my right hand attempting to grip the box and a little piece of my hair sticking up above the height of the box. She exclaimed in a loud and curious tone, "What are you doing?" My numerously repeated response, between bouts of laughter was, *"What am I doing?"*

After she removed this oversized box, I told her the story and we knew this was one for the record books. We looked for, and never found the lady who just put this onto my lap without asking me if I needed assistance or even wanted this bird feeder! I am sure this stranger shared her "random act of kindness" story with her family and friends! I know I have!

Then there was the time that I was seated outside of a religious establishment, waiting by my brother Mike's car, which was parked in a handicap accessible parking spot with my handicap permit clearly showing.

Suddenly, this lady pulled into the handicap parking next to Mike's car and got out with her two young children – a little girl about five years old and a little boy who looked about three.

They walked right past me and while pointing at my wheelchair the little girl asked her mom, "What's that?" Her mom turned away from me so I decided to quickly answer the question. This is my wheelchair and I use it because I am unable to walk yet. She then pointed to the wheelchair logo on the handicap parking sign and made a comment that my chair looked like that one in the picture.

At this point, I told her that these were special parking places for people who were in wheelchairs or had difficulty walking and needed to be close to the building's entrance.

She turned again to her mom and asked, "Mom, we can all walk good, why did you park in that space?" By now, mom was looking very embarrassed and hurried both her children into the building without answering her little girl.

Of course, she had no handicap parking permit and from past experience, the general answers I get from people whom I confront about using these accessible parking spots without a permit is, "I just have to *run* into the store to get a few things, I am in a hurry!" or "You disabled people have too many parking spots already and they are always close to the entrances," or I get shown the finger followed by many an expletive.

For me, an educated mind leads to a more understanding person and thus a more accepting person.

Not long after "My Opportunity," I went to the supermarket and I was amazed by how many people would go out of their way just to avoid going down the same grocery aisle as me. One particular time there was this young boy with his mother walking towards me. The little boy started pointing at me and said in a loud kid's voice, "Why is she in a stroller?" (referring to my wheelchair) and look at her boo boo's," probably referring to my leg brace, arm brace, neck brace or eye patch. His mother suddenly grabbed him by the arm and abruptly turned around to go down another aisle to avoid me.

I wish she had approached me and allowed this little boy to speak to me directly so I could tell him my story and hopefully educate him and his mother about people with disabilities and people in wheelchairs. Children are so curious and most people that have challenges are more than willing to share their stories so as to broaden our general acceptance from others and to dispel a lot of the untruths and rumours about people in wheelchairs. I think this would lessen the finger pointing, staring and whispering while promoting understanding and acceptance.

I often wonder what lasting impression was left in the mind of this little curious boy – *could it be that people in wheelchairs should be avoided?*

There are some times, thankfully not too many, that I am willing to accept assistance and have someone push me in my wheelchair. This one particular time, we were in Atlanta, Georgia for the Paralympic Trials.

We entered the lobby of the hotel and I was so tired and my body was hurting a lot from riding that day, that I accepted Tammy's offer to push me on the carpeted area. She was gently pushing me while chatting to the other equestrians around us when suddenly BANG. There was a second of absolute silence after that loud thud and then Tammy came running after me to see if I was alright. Yes, I had drifted down this gentle slope into a wooden pillar. Tammy was so involved in her conversation that she let go of pushing my chair and did not tell me that I was "on my own" now.

I was not paying attention to where we were going, as I thought Tammy was in the driver's seat. Everyone just started laughing with us. Neither the wooden pillar nor wheelchair were hurt during this adventure.

Now, if I let anyone push me, they totally understand my *wheelchair etiquette* and know that they have to tell me that I am "on my own" if they let go of my chair – this is for the safety of all wooden pillars and for anyone else around us.

**Helen and I having a good laugh
– wheelchair humour!**
Texas

Sense of Humour

I have found that having a sense of humour and being able to laugh at myself is the most freeing and healing of experiences. I think I have a contagious laugh and this also puts other people around me at ease and reduces their fears and ignorance of someone in a wheelchair.

Even though I did not make the Equestrian Team for the 2000 Paralympic Games, I travelled to Sydney, Australia to watch and support our team. I was staying with my good friends Pam and Chris. In fact, Pam and I met 20 years earlier in Tel Aviv, while playing field hockey for the country of Israel. We made a pact at that time in 1980, to meet again 20 years later, in the year 2000, in Australia. Little did we really know that this would actually happen!

While I was in Sydney, Pam took me shopping at her regular local supermarket, where she was well known. There are many food items in Sydney that I had not enjoyed since leaving Africa, as they are not available in Dallas. I purchased a lot of items to bring back to Texas with me, to share with my family. When we got back to her car, after loading all the bags in the back seat, she was standing by the boot (trunk) of her car while I did my usual thing of loading my wheelchair. I like to load my own chair and I can do it easily and single-handedly. I must add that it was also a very busy time at the supermarket and I decided to have a little fun with her and show her that I still had my great sense of humour.

While loading my wheelchair I shouted out in a loud voice, "Please be nice to me Pam, don't make me load my own wheelchair, I promise to be a good girl." She started saying hush and shut-up in a quiet voice and gave me *that look*. I continued to make promises of being a good girl if she would just HELP ME. By now a huge crowd was gathering around us, watching me attempt to load my wheelchair while she, a very able-bodied person, was just standing there doing nothing! No one in the crowd, including some of the store people who knew Pam, did anything at all. They just stood there unsure of how to handle what appeared to be a delicate situation. I really had to stay focused to keep a straight face through all this. Once my chair was loaded and we were back in her car, we both started laughing until tears were streaming down our faces.

Pam told me that it took her several months before she was comfortable enough to return to that supermarket without the fear of being recognized as the able-bodied person who did nothing to help her friend load the wheelchair.

Deb *down under* with the wallabies. *Australia*

It is fascinating to me to see the look on peoples' faces around us when I do this bizarre behaviour - they do not know whether to help me, walk away or just stand and stare with unquenched curiosity. I have done it many times to Tammy, to my Equest coach Gail and to my little neighbour Linda. We all still laugh every time I do it - laughter is the best medicine.

More Funny True Stories:

While staying with Rosa in Aspen, having just skied for the very first time, I was exhausted and fell asleep on the couch next to Tammy, who was watching TV. My neck was not feeling very comfortable in that position so I thought I would just pull my left arm, which would move my shoulder and in turn get my neck more comfortable. I started to pull gently on my left arm to no avail, so I pulled a little harder and then a little harder still.

I am always ready with my video camera. *South Africa*

I noticed through my sleepy eyes, that each time I would pull my arm, Tammy's head would nod forward - she asked me what I was doing? In a sleepy voice, I explained that I was pulling on my arm to get my shoulder and neck in a better position, but I was getting no relief. She started to laugh out loud and told me that the reason I was getting no relief was that I was pulling on *her arm* and not mine. You see, I have no feeling in my left arm so I did not know that it was her arm I was pulling on.

Then there was the time that Lynn and I were at a National Paralympic Dressage competition in New Jersey. After a long day in the arena, a large group of us went to a local restaurant for dinner. Upon entering the restaurant, there was a sign that read: "Please stand here to be seated."

As Lynn and I are both in wheelchairs, we could not oblige or honour this sign, so we asked to see the manager. After a few minutes, the manager came over to us. He looked very defensive and ready to deal with our complaint. We told him his sign was discriminating and as much as we liked to play by the rules, we just could not do this. Both Lynn and I were able to keep from laughing while the manager thought about what we said – he obviously took our complaint seriously. Then we started to laugh and he was so relieved when he got our joke that he too joined in the laughter.

We were just having a little bit of harmless fun. We enjoyed a great meal and several times during the course of dinner, the manager would come over to check on us or smile this great toothy smile from across the restaurant.

For me, having a sense of humour is like being driven around in a luxury car with great suspension - without the suspension, we would feel every pebble, dip and pot-hole on our journey.

~

It is a great learning experience for me, to remember that even though we are speaking the same language, interpretation can be drastically different. Two words that I use a lot are "just now." These words are often misinterpreted and taken quite literally.

I remember being at a restaurant and the waiter came to the table to get our order. He asked me if I was ready and I replied, "Just now, thank you." I expected him to walk away and return in a few minutes and yet he just stood there. Again, I repeated, "Thank you, I will order just now," and again he remained standing over me.

**I was zipping through life as a
ropes challenge course instructor. *Texas***

So, taking responsibility for my communication, I changed my response to, "Please give me a few minutes to make a decision about my order." He started laughing and replied, "The reason I never left is that the words, *just now* means right now or immediately, so I was standing ready to take your order."

I have also learnt over time, that in order to get exactly what I want at a restaurant, I am very specific with my choices. I am accustomed to saying tea and getting a cup of hot tea and yet over here in Texas, when you order tea, you get a huge glass of iced tea. When I ask for tomato sauce, I am wanting ketchup not sliced tomatoes. Little ice in my drink is not referring to the size of the ice chips. I am requesting a small amount of ice in my glass. I have since learnt to say *easy ice*. The list goes on and on....

I encourage you to find what makes you laugh and continue to *"RideStrong Through Life's Journey!"*

It is the Thought that Counts

The way we think *will* affect our daily outcomes. I was not a big fan of doing the laundry and this was beginning to become a hassle for me and a day of the week that I was dreading. Then one day I was thinking about all the clothes stuck in the clothes hamper and how they feel about laundry day. I started to laugh out loud at the thought of this being the best day of the week for the clothes - they get to leave their dark crowded smelly hamper and venture out into the washing machine where they get spun around in warm water with lots of bubbles - like dancing at a nightclub. The socks get to hold hands with the shirts and the jeans got to boogie with the sweaters. What a wonderful time they have. Then into the dryer which is like a roller coaster ride - up and down and side to side in this warm environment with a great smelling piece of lint cloth to enhance their senses. This different perspective allows me to enjoy laundry day and get me giggling every time I do another load of washing. Changing our thoughts *will* change our view of the entire day. Getting our thoughts aligned and arranging our minds, *will* allow our thoughts to manifest into reality

When my youngest nephew Adam, now a Police officer, was very young, he had an issue with going to school on Mondays. He said that he did not like Mondays. So, in order to make it easier for him, I suggested that he change Mondays to Fundays instead. This changed his negative thoughts into more positive ones. It was amazing how over time, each time Monday would roll around, he would talk of it as Funday and smile. It did not take long before he attended school every Funday through Friday and enjoyed each and every day. Adam is now happily married to Arielle, they have a beautiful son and they are expecting a daughter in the New Year.

(l-r) Adam, Elijah and Arielle. *Texas*

Positive and loving thoughts create positive and uplifting emotions, which result in positive action and movement. This keeps us going in the right direction. Negative thoughts create negative emotions, which results in negative actions or worse, no action at all, thus keeping us stuck in a situation. Our thoughts are one thing that we get to choose for ourselves every minute of every day!

I get to meet so many different people from all walks of life in many different countries and I have found that a lot of people that I meet appear more paralyzed in their minds than I am in my physical body.

Look inside yourself, hear your thoughts, feel your emotions and become your own catalyst for change. A simple change in a thought pattern can influence your every action and allow you to propel yourself fully into life. Something that has always fascinated me is that when I make a change in myself, the entire world around me appears to change. Do it and enjoy it – just something to think about!

I love the statement by Henry Ford,
"Whether you think you can, or you think you can't, you're right."

Another story here is when I was at the Paralympics in Sydney Australia. Pam and I were watching the finals of women's wheelchair basketball. We had premium seats and were thoroughly enjoying this amazing event. We had not been seated very long when a security guard came over to me and asked if I was feeling ok. I replied, "Yes thank you," and he moved on. Not too long after that he came back and asked me if I needed anything – I told him that I was quite fine, and again he left me alone. He came back a third and fourth time and asked very politely if I needed help finding the rest rooms. Again, I thanked him for his kindness and told him that we just wanted to enjoy the game.

By now, both Pam and I were really intrigued by the attention I was getting and almost annoyed at being interrupted so many times. I finally wheeled my chair back to go and ask another security guard what was going on when I saw "it"….. yes, "it" was all over the concrete floor. The "it" I am referring to is a huge puddle of Fanta orange juice that spilled from my can, under my wheelchair. As I have reduced feeling on my left side, I had no idea that the can had tipped over and "it" was slowly dripping off my seat. By now you can also understand why the security guard had been so attentive to me – we all know what that orange puddle under my wheelchair must have looked like!

I am sure that the security guard also realized that
it is the thought that counts.

**Sweet MaMa Jo and Sylvia. Sunset Lake in Hunstville -
where MaMa Jo and Gwapie Jen got me fishing again after
"My Opportunity."** *Texas*

Self-Motivation, Trust and Attitude

Life is in a perpetual and continuous state of change – a hard reality sometimes and yet if we think about it, it is actually a good thing. Without change, we would still be toddlers that were not potty trained or young adolescents with raging hormones. We would still have to get up and change the TV channels and adjust the rabbit-ear antenna to get a better signal. Oh, so many changes in our lives and I look at them all as transitions. Nothing lasts forever so we transition from one to another.

It is during these periods of transition that we can find what motivates us, what moves us, what gets us up every morning. Are we motivated by the concept of the carrot on a stick or the whip? Do we move towards pleasure (the carrot) or away from pain (the whip)? Do you operate out of desire and forward movement or do you operate out of avoidance and fear? Do you move towards your goals to achieve your outcomes or do you move towards your goals to avoid pain or unpleasant experiences?

An example of this would be: I am going to train as hard as I can to make the team, so I can ride in the Olympic Stadium or... I am going to train as hard as I can to make the team to avoid feeling like a failure and endure the painful ridicule from my peers.

I am definitely motivated by the carrot. I love moving towards my goals and for me, self-motivation begins with trust. Trust in one's inner-self and one's abilities. Now a lot of people claim to have trust issues, trusting no one and nothing including themselves. Well, this may be true and yet I wonder if they have ever thought about how trusting they really are each and every day.

They get out of bed daily – a bed that is held together with nails and screws. Before they get into bed, do they check every nail and screw to ensure that they are working or do they trust that the bed will hold together while they get some shut-eye? The same goes for their car – no one checks their vehicles every time before driving to ensure that every screw, nut and bolt, tire and wire is holding perfectly together! No… we get into the car trusting that it will get us where we are going. We sit in unknown chairs at a restaurant and have unquestionable trust that the seat will remain screwed to the legs while we enjoy our meal.

These are just a few examples of trust that most of us encounter each and every day. Now if we could only take that same level of trust and apply it in a clear positive way to get self-motivated.

I went to Disney World in Florida for the first time with Tammy. She was amazing how she was able to assist me to get through the myriad of people roaming around. It is fascinating how many people just look out at eye level and not see anything lower down, like ME. I have had drinks spilled on me, popcorn dropped on me, people running into my wheelchair and even people who just climbed over me like a stepping stone, occasionally landing in my lap!

Well, we were enjoying our day at Disney when Tammy took me over to a ride called "Space Mountain." I was curious about this ride and when I asked Tammy about it, her response was, "You will enjoy this ride." I trusted her and thought we were going on a slow sightseeing ride to see the entire Disney World theme park from atop the mountain.

When we got to the front of the line, (which is a shorter wait for wheelchair users,) I see what looks like a roller coaster ride, with single seating one behind another. I wheel towards the ride and Tammy is going to assist me in transferring into one of the seats. I wanted to sit behind her so I could grab her shoulder if I needed some support. I was not sure how a complete stranger would take to me gripping *their* shoulder! Tammy insisted that I sit in front of her and even though I was protesting, she was adamant about our seating positions.

Still none the wiser about this ride, I agreed to sit in front of her because I trust her. We are buckled in with our seat belts and this ride starts off nice and gentle, slowly on the tracks. We quickly enter a dark area and now I am concerned. I can hear Tammy behind me and she has a hand on my shoulder. The next thing, we are increasing speed and there are flashing lights and this becomes a superfast roller coaster ride. I just had to laugh or else I would have started to cry. I have a fear of high speed roller coasters and yet here I was, about to experience my first major roller coaster ride! I could feel the adrenaline pumping through my body and my mind was racing!

We picked up speed and the roller coaster would go up and down, up and down and then make sharp turns to either side. Up and down was not an issue for me, turns to the right were no worries either, as I could prop myself up with my right arm. Then I had a flash of fear as I realized this ride was going to make a sharp left and without the use of my left arm, I had no way of balancing myself as I slumped over to that side.

Then it became super clear to me, as to why Tammy had insisted on sitting behind me. She had been on this ride before and knew what she had to do to keep me safe and comfortable. When we started to veer off to the left side, I could feel her behind me, holding onto my shoulders as we tilted left, balancing me and then guiding me back into an upright position.

What a rush this was. I would never have volunteered for this ride on Space Mountain if I had known what it was about and yet, I rode through my fear and came out the other side, unscathed, turning that fear into an opportunity for courage. I am so excited to have done it! I use this experience as a way to motivate myself in many areas of my life, especially in situations where I experience fear!

I am so grateful to Tammy for allowing me to access that excitement, exhilaration and courage and for letting me experience TOTAL TRUST!

Tammy and I enjoying our holiday. *Florida*

Start trusting in yourself to make the best decisions you can make. Start trusting that you can achieve anything you put your mind to. After "My Opportunity," due to my dependency on so many people to help me, my level of trust had to grow and expand with each passing hour. It was through this trust that I am motivated to become more independent.

Sometimes, being self-motivated is difficult. If I encounter a day like that, then I think about how I would encourage my best friend to get motivated. What would I say to enable them to trust themselves again and get motivated for that day? After I think about that for a while, I use that same encouragement on myself.

To be self-motivated we also need to fan the flames of desire within our soul, to find the emotions that spark us into action. A lot of this has to do with our attitude.

I once read this interesting article on attitude, and it goes like this:

"Look at the numerical position of each letter in the word **attitude** with relation to their position in the alphabet. A being 1, B being 2, C being 3 all the way to Z being 26.

A = 1 T= 20 T= 20 I= 9 T=20 U=21 D=4 E=5

Now add these together and what do you get? 100. Confirming that your attitude is 100% your responsibility! Attitude is power."

The more responsibility you take in running your life and the more you trust yourself, the more self-motivated you will become and the happier and more positive you will stay. You will be more in control of all the different ways to motivate yourself to reach your outcomes and desired goals, and to become the best YOU, that you can be!

I have been involved in many competitions and won many local and national equestrian titles. The awards, blue ribbons, belt buckles and trophies are fantastic, exciting and definitely an adrenaline high and yet the greatest part of all of this for me, is the fact that I continue to use these accolades to motivate myself to the next level of achievement. It is an external validation of my internal commitment to self-motivate. It is a knowing in my heart that I am a winner and letting my heart shine through in all that I do. This is brighter than any highly polished belt buckle or trophy. It is what's in your heart that makes you a champion and a winner - not the trophy or the medal.

I can be a better me than I can be anyone else.

I am my biggest and only competition
in the areas of my life that really count.

Saddled with Backache to Back in the Saddle

After "My Opportunity," I went through many years of ever increasing back problems. Finally I was able to have surgery on my spine to get some relief from the excruciating pain that was so debilitating. This major surgery forced me to take two years off from my equestrian endeavours.

My first "back in the saddle" horse competition was in Fort Worth, Texas at the Chisholm Challenge Competition for Equestrians with Disabilities. There were over 100 riders, from many different Therapeutic facilities, that competed in various competitions over a three-day period.

It felt so good to go from being *"saddled with backache to back in the saddle,"* and I was welcomed back into the arena of competition by so many of my friends, riders, coaches and volunteers.

On my first day of competition, I placed first in both of my events and received a great looking belt buckle and a blue ribbon. At the end of my ride, just before I was to dismount Zena, the husband of one of the coaches from another therapeutic facility, came over to congratulate me and welcome me back to this competition. He was amazed at how straight and upright I was sitting in the saddle and commented on this several times during our two-minute conversation.

I told him that I had undergone major back surgery, an anterior-posterior 360-degree spinal fusion of my lower back with lots of hardware (rods and screws) inserted in my spine. He jokingly asked if that was the reason for my great posture! At this point, I motioned for him to get closer to me as though I wanted to tell him a big secret. He leaned in close and I quietly told him that I had a heavy-duty magnet placed inconspicuously into my saddle by my saddle-maker, so that when I mounted my horse, the force of the magnets in conjunction with the rods and screws in my lower back, pulled me into the perfectly straight upright-seated position. I kept a very straight face while telling him this, even though I was laughing like a little girl on the inside.

While telling him this, I noticed that his eyes were getting bigger and bigger, looking like saucers on his face! He then asked me in a whisper, "Is that legal?" and "Do the judges know about this?" I just smiled, sat upright in my saddle and waited to be dismounted into my wheelchair by my coach Gail. The only thing I said to him after that was, "Now you know why I have a magnetic personality!"

Word got around the entire barn very quickly and over the next couple of days, I had several coaches and other riders come and ask me if they could see my magical magnetic saddle. Many of them even asked for the name and phone number of my saddle-maker who had done such a good job for me! I also noticed how many more people were suddenly watching me mount Zena during practice sessions and before I would compete in my events!

At this particular competition, for safety reasons, none of the riders are allowed into the barn area where our horses are stabled and our tack is stored. Only our coaches and volunteers can enter this area. Many of my Equest volunteers and especially our barn manager Carol, told me that several coaches and family members of some of the riders, would nonchalantly wander into the Equest tack room to look at, inspect and even feel the saddle owned by Deb Lewin. Of course, all my coaches and volunteers were in on this funny story and none of them let on about the joke!

Zena and I were magnetically connected. *Texas*

Before the last day of competition had ended, I made sure that everyone knew this was just a "magnetic myth" and that there really were no magnets in my saddle. This story made many people laugh out loud and some of them were actually embarrassed that they had ever believed such a story. Many of them proceeded to tell me how they would sneak into the Equest tack room to look at my saddle and some of them were even taking pictures of my saddle and tack. To this day, I laugh out loud when I share this story.

I reminded all my fellow equestrians that it was many, many hours of hard work, dedication and exercise that had me sitting in a perfectly straight upright-seated position - none of which would be possible without the dedicated staff, volunteers and amazing horses at our therapeutic riding facilities.

"RideStrong Through Life's Journey!"

We all Know what Assume Does!!

After working and living in Richardson for four years, I knew I was truly integrated into the American way of life when I went back to South Africa for a visit and to teach some classes in NLP.

While in Johannesburg, we made plans to meet some friends down town and then go and enjoy a meal together. It was their suggestion that we meet at McDonald's at 11:30am. Easy enough I thought - those golden arches can be seen for miles so I knew I would not get lost. I was also curious to see the layout of a McDonald's in Africa, as they did not have one when I lived there. We left the house a little earlier so as not to be caught in traffic and as we were driving there, we remembered that unlike Dallas, the traffic here was really very mild.

We arrived at the street in question and started looking for the golden arches - we drove up and down and up again. There were no golden arches, no Mickey "D's," no pictures of a Big Mac to be seen anywhere.

Finally, we stopped to ask a pedestrian and we were directed to a parking lot and told that McDonald's was around the corner. Great! We parked the car, paid the parking lot attendant and headed to our arranged meeting place. Again, no arches to be seen.

Then we saw a painted sign on the brick face of the building and just started laughing so hard. It read, Macdonalds - Home of Fine men's clothing & haberdashery since nineteen hundred and something.

We were so used to using McDonald's and the golden arches as landmarks in the USA that we had no reason to assume otherwise. It was then that I knew I was becoming an American and I got to experience the real meaning behind ass/u/me!

127

Mom and I rolling around Manhatten. *New York*

Skiing in Aspen - This is How I Roll

During the skiing part of my involvement in the documentary film "From Fear to Faith – Ordinary People, ExtraOrdinary Lives," Tammy and I stayed with Rosa in her magnificent house, up on the hill in Aspen, Colorado.

Unaccustomed to snow, ice and freezing temperatures, I ventured outside the house in my wheelchair to the driveway to demonstrate to Tammy what I learnt that day in my first skiing lesson. She had the video camera with her as she was taping the beautiful sunset over the Colorado mountains. She kept the camera rolling as I came down the driveway going right then left then right again in a zig zag pattern, feeling proud that I could show off my newly learnt skills.

Well... with no depth perception and no idea that the drive way was a solid block of ice, it only took a few seconds before I lost traction and lost control of my wheelchair and just started sliding down towards the snow banked side walk. I gained great momentum down this very steep driveway and went flying head first into the 4-foot bank of snow on the side. It was a soft landing and I just lay there, laughing out loud from my belly. Tammy had this all on tape and was laughing so much that she could hardly keep the camera steady. Between loud bursts of laughter, she commented on how it looked like I was lying face down in the fluffy soft snow with a wheelchair glued to my butt and the wheels of the chair were still spinning. That comment got us both laughing even more. We laughed so hard that our bellies ached and the tears rolling down our cheeks felt like frozen droplets on our faces.

It took several minutes before we gained enough composure and strength, to get me out of the snow and back into my now ice-packed and frozen wheelchair. Tammy then had the wondrous task of pushing me back up this steep icy drive way and into the house. That in itself was another opportunistic experience - each time we laughed, we would slide backwards!

If while reading this, you can picture the scenario, you too will be laughing by now. Every time I show this video to friends or use it in my motivational speaking engagements, everyone, including myself, gets to laugh out loud. This is one of the funniest and most exhilarating experiences of my life and really emphasizes one of the philosophies that I live by:

"It is not about the cards I am dealt in life,
it is about how I play the game with the cards that I am dealt,
that ultimately determines my happiness in life."

I am bundled up, strapped in and excited for my first skiing experience. *Colorado*

Follow Me Mom

We went on a girl's weekend trip to Las Vegas a few years ago. There was my Mom, Tammy, Mom Billie, our Tia Peaches and Dr. Pam. Mom and I each rented electric scooters from the casino, so we could get around more easily and be more independent. My manual wheelchair causes a lot of pain in my body when I have to manoeuvre over carpet, especially the plush Vegas style casino carpeting.

We always have such a great time together, especially when we all play the slot machines in close proximity to each other. In fact, none of us drink alcohol and yet everyone around thinks we are drunk because we are all having such a fantastic time. Really, all it takes is one winning cherry on a penny slot machine to get us all riled up, laughing and joking out loud.

Vegas Girls (l-r) Mom, Mom Billie, Dr. Pam, Tammy, Tia Peaches and myself. *Nevada*

Well, this Saturday afternoon, after playing in the casino, we all decided to use the "little girls" room before leaving our hotel to do some sightseeing.

This hotel, like most casino hotels, had several restrooms along the walls, around the outskirts of the casino area, with the men's restroom on the right and the women's adjacent on the left side.

I knew where it was, so I said, *"Follow me Mom,"* and off we scooted, through the crowds and towards the back wall where one set of restrooms were located. We were in convoy with me leading, Mom behind me, followed by Tammy, Mom Billie, Tia Peaches and Dr. Pam.

We were all laughing and chatting and of course, not paying attention. After all, we had done these restroom trips several times that weekend already!

Well, I proceeded toward the restroom on the left and entered on my scooter followed by Mom and the rest of the girls. Was I surprised when the first thing I saw were the men's urinals and several men at the hand basins! Then I heard this deep male voice exclaiming, "Hey what the *"bleep"* are you doing in here?"

By this time it was too late to stop our entourage from entering. I know my eyes got as large as saucers when I stopped my scooter so suddenly and Mom had to swerve her scooter towards the urinals so as not to run into me or anyone else for that matter. The excitement that followed goes something like this; male voices hollering, cheering and laughing; girly shrieks and gasps from some of our group; the swishing sound from the urinals and toilets flushing; the beep beep back-up scooter noises from Mom and me trying to reverse our scooters and of course, non-stop laughter.

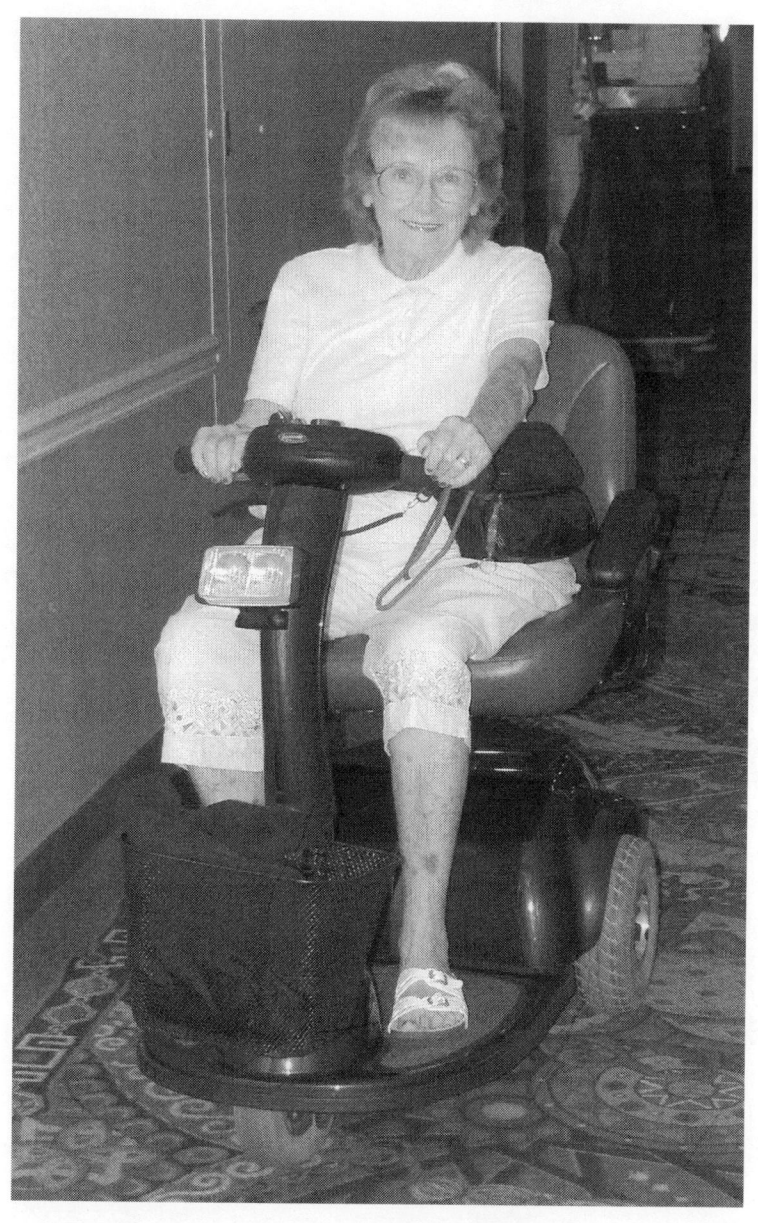

Mom styling in her scooter in Vegas. *Nevada*

We finally all made it out of the men's restroom and went next door to the ladies' restrooms. It is a good thing that we all had great bladder control or we would have needed more than just the restrooms! You could say that this was a different version of, "Texas hold-em."

Upon entering our gender designated restrooms, the ladies in there were chatting out loud about how two men had entered just minutes before. It turns out that these two guys were following our group so when our entourage of girls entered the restrooms on the left, they automatically entered the restrooms on the right, also paying no attention to the signage.

When we composed ourselves, and stopped crying from laughing so hard, we wandered around the outskirts of the casino and took note of all the restrooms. Every combination of men's and ladies' restrooms had men to the right and ladies to the left. The only restroom layout that was different was the one we wandered into. Talk about hitting the jackpot – another lucky day at that casino.

Our Shooting Star

It was one o'clock in the morning when Tammy and I were finally heading home from fishing at the marina with Marty & Nan. We were driving on highway 22 by Lake Whitney when suddenly Tammy said she saw something moving on the side of the highway. She slowed way down and did a U-turn.

Pulling up slowly, she realized that it was a horse, loose on the side of the highway, just grazing! She put on her car blinkers and started to follow this little guy as he was wandering along the grassy sidewalk. Even though this is a 2-lane blacktop highway, it had no centreline dividers or side rails. The highway meets the grassy verge and then there are some fences and private property mixed in with business entrances.

At this point, I called 911 and reported our dilemma. Meanwhile, Tammy is driving very slowly abreast of the horse, attempting to keep him on the grassy verge and off the highway! She kept the emergency flashers on and flashed her bright lights to warn all the other drivers to slow way down as there was something going on and we didn't want to spook this horse.

Suddenly, this *"yahoo"* in his pickup truck starts to overtake us at high speed, pulls in front of us and immediately had to slam on his brakes, just missing the horse by inches. We also had to stop abruptly to avoid hitting his pickup truck!

Of course, this spooked the horse and he moved from the side grassy verge and started trotting down the highway. Clippity-clop, clippity-clop. We heard the sound of his shoes so we knew he had an owner and was somebody's pet or working horse and not a wild horse in the middle of this country town.

Tammy continued to follow the horse, attempting to get him off the highway and yet he continued trotting faster and faster and wandered over onto the oncoming side of the highway. Tammy followed him over to that opposite side of the highway, as there was no oncoming traffic at the time.

After about a mile of harrowing, heart stopping moments, Tammy was able to use her car to guide him down into the grassy verge area, where he started grazing again. She pulled into a nearby entrance and as we got out of the car, we both saw the same shooting star!

Naturally, we named this horse "Shooting Star." He was a small thin brown horse with one white sock on his back left leg and a full white blaze down his face.

We made a moving human/car blockade to keep him in the grassy area waiting for the police officer to show up. It was a very dark night, with only a small half-moon behind the clouds and no streetlights at all. I was using my fishing flashlight on the highway to notify all the 18-wheelers and speeding cars, to slow down and to become aware of Tammy and me on the side of the highway.

About 30 minutes later, this wonderful young highway deputy shows up. He told us that he was raised on a farm in that neighbourhood so we started to feel good thinking that he knew how to handle this situation – he then proceeded to tell us he knew everything about cows and nothing about horses. He called for backup and his partner is supposedly on his way to help us and bring us some rope to secure our "Shooting Star." After a while, we get notified that the other deputy was now dealing with a DWI and could not assist the three of us. Again, "Shooting Star" started to wander up towards the highway.

So, with no rope or the assistance of another deputy, we had to come up with another plan. We got our three dog leashes out of the car and Tammy and the deputy slowly made their way towards the horse, while I continued to use my flashlight to warn traffic. They finally got close enough to touch him and talk to him in a calm fashion.

Everything Tammy knows about horses, she learnt from EQUEST – what a blessing that information was. Slowly, slowly, they were able to lay one of the dog leashes onto the neck of "Shooting Star," then loop it and make a lead rope out of it. "Shooting Star" was ok with this and yet when the deputy attempted to lead him, he became as stubborn as a mule and would not budge.

After much coaxing and tempting him with long green grass, Tammy and the deputy were able to get "Shooting Star" to an area where he could happily graze while we secured him to a fence. This fence was the perimeter of a boat repair company and I could tell that "Shooting Star" had never been this close to boats and boat engines before, yet he handled it very well.

We continued to watch over "Shooting Star" for about three more hours. We talked to him, petted him and kept him calm while the deputy drove around the country side attempting to locate the owner or even a fenced in pasture that we could get the horse into for the remainder of the night – no such luck!

Finally around 6am, the owner was located and "Shooting Star" was able to go home safe and sound, as were we. The next day, this wonderful deputy called us and met up with Tammy to return our dog leashes. We always carry dog leashes in our car as we find so many stray dogs – perhaps we need to carry a lead rope and halter in our vehicle as well!

What a G-D wink it was, that Tammy noticed this loose horse. We got to wish upon our *"Shooting Star"* and our wishes, to prevent a possible disaster on the highway for both horse and human, were granted.

We met in Old San Juan - Theodore Roosevelt (Memorial).
Puerto Rico

Mistaken Identity

Once a week, early in the morning, Tammy would drop me off on her way to work and I would sit and wait patiently for about half an hour for my coach Gail to pick me up and take me to Equest for our weekly riding lesson.

Tammy and Gail had figured out a central drop off location for me that was accessible for both of them on their routes to work. This particular location was at a cross road of a major highway. It wasn't until my first drop off there that I found out it was the parking lot for an assisted living facility for residents with Alzheimer's disease.

So, every week I would wait in the parking lot for Gail to show up in her big diesel truck. This one particular morning, it was very cold and windy and I was dressed appropriately in a thick wind breaker jacket with the hoodie secured tightly around my face. I had my backpack on the back of my wheelchair, my riding saddle which was covered in a thick waterproof zippered cover was on my lap and my duffle bag, filled with riding tack, was sitting by my right wheel. I had parked myself under some shelter and behind a brick column for protection from the wind.

This same morning, a lady approached me and asked me my name. I was polite and told her. She asked me what I had in my lap and again, I told her. She commented that I was in a wheelchair and could not possibly ride horses, so it was best for me to come back into the building and she would help me find my room.

I explained that I was waiting for my coach to come and get me and take me to Equest for my horse therapy and again she was very kind and polite and suggested that it was best for me to get out of the cold weather and return to my room inside this assisted living facility.

Once again, I told her I did not live there. I continued to tell her again that this was the mutual meeting place for Tammy to drop me off and for Gail to pick me up. She nodded her head politely, made the "uh huh" sound several times while attempting to pick up my duffle bag and coax me into wheeling myself towards the entrance of the building. Again I verbalized my situation to her and this time her response was, "Don't make me have to holler for security to get you back to your room honey, let's just get back into the warm building."

This ordeal went on for several minutes until Gail finally drove up in her diesel truck. She got out of the truck to help me load my stuff and was dressed in horse riding gear with an Equest logo on her shirt.

At this point, the lady apologized profusely and explained that I looked very suspicious sitting all bundled up in my generic wheelchair, with my face mostly covered by my hoodie and a bag on my lap. All the attendants and staff were trained to be on the lookout for patients who may have wandered off.

Even though this was a case of mistaken identity, it was better to be safe than sorry. I thanked this lady for her kindness and dedication to the residents at that facility, then we all had a good laugh before Gail and I headed off to Equest.

Fire Drill – Not for us Foreigners!

Equest offers an Instructor Training Course where people come from all over the world to get certified as therapeutic riding instructors. There is a lot of classroom work required by the new students as well as many hours of "hands-on" training with the horses and riders.

This particular day I agreed to work with the class of new student instructors. They were learning many different ways of mounting and dismounting a rider as well as the different positions their volunteers would assist in, like leading the horse or being a side-walker as a safety factor for the rider.

Our Instructor Gail showed the group how she had developed an interesting way of getting me mounted, using my left leg to hoist me up high and with the strength of my right hand, I would hold onto the safety handle and lower myself easily into the saddle. Of course, we omitted to mention how many times Gail nearly threw me completely *over* the horse due to her strength and my enthusiasm.

We proceeded to enter the covered arena from the mounting area. I now had three student instructors with me. One at the front of the horse leading us around and one on either side of me as side-walkers. There were four other horse and rider teams with their new student instructors, all going through the same exercises with Gail.

Gail proceeded to explain certain aspects and requirements of these different positions and wanted each student to experience every position for themselves. She also wanted to reiterate that at no time was the rider to be left alone. Then she said, "OK, Fire Drill."

No one in my team moved. I looked at my student instructors; they were looking at me, then looking at each other then looking back at me. Gail, now looking at our group specifically, repeated, "Fire Drill" and again no one in my group moved. We noticed all the other groups were moving and yet none of us seemed to understand what she was asking us to do.

You see, I am from Africa and my three student instructors were also from foreign countries, so none of us understood this game of "Fire Drill," which involves moving and changing positions.

When Gail used her best instructor voice to say "Fire Drill," her expected outcome, was for each student instructor to move around the horse to experience a different position.

I can still hear Gail laughing from the belly when she finally realized that none of us knew what to do as we had never played this game before.

Fire Drill – Not for us Foreigners!

Tales, Straight from the Horses' Mouth

When I first started going out to Equest to ride, I had no horse experience at all. It was all new to me, especially the horse lingo and all the riding equipment that I needed to learn about:

Riding helmets,

Bridles,

Saddles,

Bits,

Reins,

Girths,

Safety handles,

Tack room,

Grooms for the horses and so on and so forth.

I was into the discipline of dressage which requires English riding equipment and I had not seen a tack store in our city. There were a few stores in surrounding cities that carried tack for western saddles so any equipment that I needed, was purchased on the internet or through magazines from places up north where english riding is the main equestrian discipline.

One morning before I went to Equest for my lesson, I was listening to the radio and I got so very excited when I heard a radio commercial about "bridal accessories and gifts for the groom." I thought that a new tack store was coming to my city of Richardson. I had to rein in my enthusiasm, when that commercial ended by repeating the name of this new *wedding super store* opening soon!

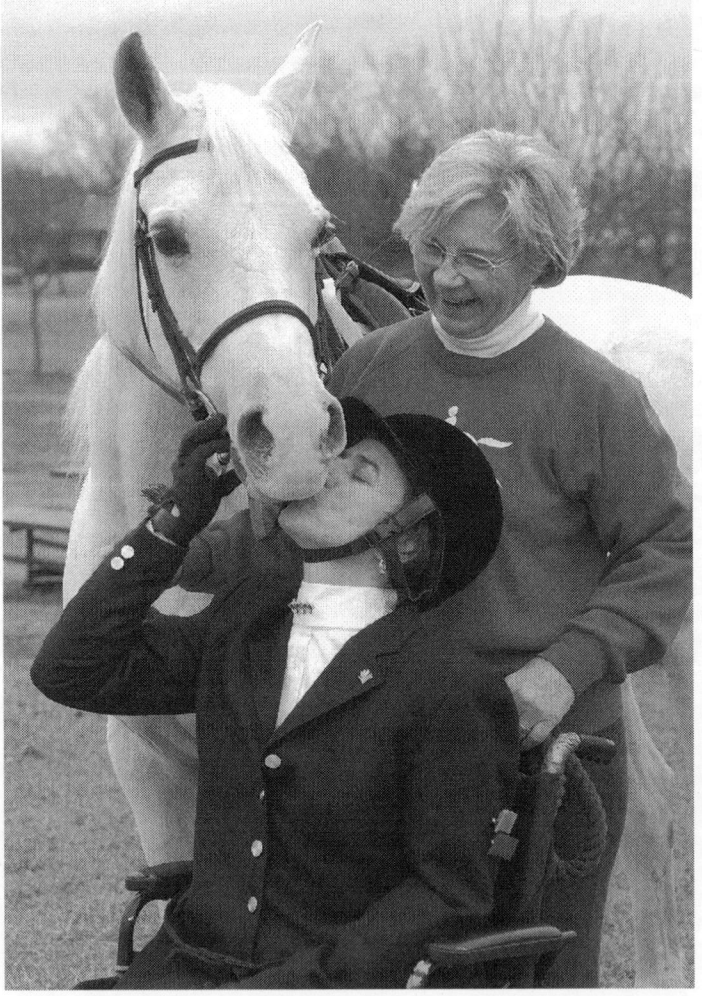

NB_29MILLER#63100 Cheryl Diaz Meyer/The Dallas Morning News

The terrific trio of Deb, Gail and Zena. *Texas*

Tammy has really taught me a lot about living in the moment. She has a wonderful child-like curiosity and makes me laugh. When she was driving me around, she would often drive me close to the curb if she saw a sprinkler system on. She would slow down when we got close to the sprinklers and then open my window all the way down and laugh as the water droplets would get me through the open window.

In that particular car, the window controls were in the middle console between the two front seats and by the time I could reach around with my right arm to raise my window up again, we were long past the sprinklers. This happened so many times and yet we would just laugh each and every time.

Tammy pushed me all over this private island in this PVC waterproof wheelchair. Too cool! *Bahamas*

One summer during a dressage lesson at Equest, Zena, the beautiful Arabian mare that I was riding, refused to go down the long rail and kept turning towards the middle of the arena. I used every cue and riding aid that I knew and accessed every equine move I had, to get her to go straight and nothing worked. She was determined and very adamant about not going towards the end of the arena.

When Gail my coach asked me what was wrong, an image of a bunny popped into my head. I told her that there was a rabbit in the far corner of the arena. Gail was skeptical at first. "How do you know that Deb, you can't even see that far?" she said. I replied, "Zena told me!" Gail agreed to walk to the end of the arena and sure enough, there was a rabbit in the far corner. Zena was protecting all of us from the dreaded bunny.

G-D's window on the Brazos River. *Texas*

146

After Gail persuaded the rabbit to leave, Zena gladly agreed to go down the long side of the arena with very little encouragement from me. Her silent words spoke volumes to me.

~

Tammy and I were working on a DIY project in the motor home. I was holding two pieces of wire and she was using pliers to tighten them together. The finger on my right hand got caught between the wires and I shouted, "Hold-on, hold-on" and she did. The louder and harder I screamed, the tighter and tighter she held on. For me, "hold-on" means stop what you are doing - for her, obviously not! Finally, I figured out that I had to change my communication to get her to let go of the wires and ultimately my finger. I did and she did. No real damage was caused by my assumption that she would understand my communication.

**Deb playing "Deep in the Heart of Texas"
on National Television. *Rhodesia***

Early on in my Equestrian life, there were very, very few competitions that riders with disabilities were allowed to enter. We could only do demonstrations, which I did on a regular basis with one of Equest's amazing horses and my coach Gail.

I was part of the Equest Quadrille Team (four riders) where we would enter the arena, already mounted and do a synchronized dressage demonstration to music. When we were done riding our routine, we halted in the middle of the arena and saluted our audience. They would in turn clap for us. Then, our volunteers would enter with our wheelchairs, walkers, crutches or whatever assistive devices we used when not riding.

We were assisted off our horses and then suddenly the crowds would stand up and really cheer for us and clap thunderously. Most of the audience had no idea what challenges we had while we were riding. We wanted them to acknowledge our ability to ride and control our horses before they knew what challenges we were overcoming.

It took a few years of doing demonstrations only, before most of the big able-bodied dressage shows allowed us to compete. It is a fantastic feeling to have been at the grassroots level of this major change in the Equestrian world. Now, there are competitions for riders with disabilities at every major able-bodied horse show. We were able to change *Impossible to I'm Possible.*

My catch of the day on Lake Whitney. *Texas*

I was speaking to my elder brother Trev on the phone the other day and even though he is mentally challenged, he has such an incredible outlook on life. We finished chatting and I ended the conversation with *"Have a good day at work tomorrow"* to which he replied, *"I know I will."* Out of curiosity, I asked him how he knew that.

He proceeded to tell me that every morning when he wakes up, he says *"Today I'm going to have a good day, and I do."* He makes his mind up before his day begins! I am so very proud of my brother and he never ceases to amaze me how he overcomes his daily obstacles. *How do you arrange your mind?*

If you could see you, through my eyes – you are perfect!
Texas

I am not from an equestrian family and our lack of elementary horsie knowledge was very apparent when we went to a local equine event. Laureen took her mom Gaby, my Mom and me to a horse show and I remember wandering through the barn, proudly sharing what *little* horse smarts I had recently acquired from Equest – the difference between an English and western saddle, the different kind of bits, this is a halter and this is a lead rope etc.

We passed several beautiful horses, saw some fancy tack, went into some booths that were handing out informational flyers about different horse breed organizations, watched this guy put a blinding shine onto a competitor's tall boots and then saw a table with a sign that read, "homemade all-natural cookies" (meaning *biscuits* to us). Mom and I went over there and grabbed several biscuits, each individually wrapped in clear plastic and about the size of a silver dollar. We shared our treasures with Laureen and Gaby.

We continued to wander towards the far side of the barn to go and visit our Equest horses, when I heard Laureen say to mom, "Even though these are hard and dry, they are quite tasty!" I turned around in time to see Laureen *eating* the last of her biscuit. I was gobsmacked (astounded) and started laughing so hard that I could not speak. It took a little while before she realized that she had *eaten* a horse biscuit. Even though they looked exactly like human biscuits, we were, after all, at a horse show and we should have known better. I am so glad that they were the homemade and all-natural variety of treats.

This *biscuit blunder* happened very early on in my equestrian career and yet we still laugh about it today!

I Dream of Africa

In the summer of 2013, my Uncle Salvo was celebrating his 80th birthday. For many months prior to this milestone event, I had been researching regularly on how to use my airline miles to get a ticket home to Zimbabwe, Africa to celebrate with my family. Well with the economy the way it was, the airlines were offering fewer and fewer seats in exchange for accumulated mileage. I did everything I knew how to do and finally I had to settle for the reality that I was not going to make it home for the celebration.

It was almost noon on Wednesday, Dallas time and I was sitting on my verandah (patio) talking on Skype with my cousin Nonees. I was going over my emailed speech that I wanted her to read at her Dad's birthday party. I was crying while doing this as it was very painful for me knowing that I could not be with them all at this magical time.

Tammy walked outside and motioned to me that she was going over to help Joy with a plumbing problem. Rob and Joy live a few miles away and it was not unusual for either of us to assist any of our family members that needed help.

About an hour later, she returned home and told me that she needed an extra hand with this plumbing issue. *I was glad she only needed one extra hand as I only have one fully functional one - ha ha ha.* We went back to their house and upon entering the kitchen area I saw Rob and Joy sitting at the table. I was confused as to why Rob was home during a workday. He told me that he was working from home that afternoon as he had just returned from having his medical infusion drip for his rheumatoid arthritis.

He proceeded to ask me what I was doing the next day. I told him I was waiting to hear from our other brother Trev, to see what he might need help with, as Thursdays were normally his day off from work. Trev is mentally challenged and since our Mom passed away, I assist him in all areas of his life – his paperwork and bills, phone calls, banking, medical issues, shopping etc.

"Well," Rob said, "you had better clear your schedule for the next three weeks as you are flying home to Zimbabwe tomorrow morning!"

I was in shock – it was a good thing I was sitting in my wheelchair as I would have literally fallen to the floor.

I could not believe my ears and I just started crying and having difficulty breathing due to my asthma. I took my inhaler, calmed down for a second when Tammy leaned down and said, "And I am going with you." More tears and more shortness of breath.

When I was able to compose myself, Joy reiterated that they had purchased return (round trip) tickets for both Tammy and I to fly back to Zimbabwe to celebrate Uncle Salvo's 80th birthday.

It turned out that there was no plumbing problem at Rob and Joy's house after all. That was just a pretense for Tammy to go over and get Rob's help in finding me a ticket to go home. Tammy had been looking on-line to get me a ticket home and as she knew nothing about which countries in Africa were safe to travel through, she needed Rob's help as he is a seasoned world-traveller. She said it just tore her apart when she saw me crying earlier that day, while reading my speech with Nonees, and she was going to do whatever was necessary to get me home in time.

While Tammy was over at their house, without me, she and Rob were on their iPads and laptops, searching for tickets and air routes to get me back to Africa by Sunday morning.

It was at this time that Rob asked Tammy why she was not going with me to Africa. He knew it was a dream of mine to take

Tammy back to my home in Africa and he also knew it was on our *goal reaching* board. Tammy explained that as much as she wanted to, she had a business to run, an eBay store to keep up with, our three dogs to look after and financially it was just not possible at that moment.

Rob then asked Tammy to call our Pet nanny Randa, and ask her if she was available to stay overnight with our three boys and feed them morning and night for the next three weeks. Randa was available every night except for four nights during those 21 days and on those four days she would still feed them and be with them part of each day. It was at this time that Rob hit the "purchase" button on his laptop and confirmed two tickets to Zimbabwe on Emeritus airlines.

It was now mid-afternoon on Wednesday and our flight left at 9am the following morning. We left Rob and Joy's home, went to the pharmacy to make sure that we had enough medication for our three week holiday (vacation); went to the pet store and purchased extra crunchies, canned food and treats needed for our fur-kids for the next three weeks. We also had to get to the bank before they closed to get some cash to take on our adventure. By now, we had less than 12 hours before we needed to be at the Dallas/Ft. Worth International airport to start our trip of a lifetime.

The infrastructure in Zimbabwe is such that there is no consistent electricity or running water in the cities on any given day. Knowing this, we could not take any chances of conducting our business online from there, not knowing from one hour to the next if there would be power or internet services available.

Tammy and I had to accomplish so many things before we could leave the next morning. This included and was not limited to: getting our passports and ID's ready – luckily, we did not need to have any specific vaccinations or get a visa to enter into Zimbabwe; closing our eBay store; figuring out how and when to pay our bills online; setting up all overseas activities, container shipments and wire transfers for the business; preparing several cheques and stamped envelopes to give to our little neighbor Linda to mail on certain dates; getting our cell phones activated for phone and text messaging capabilities from outside the USA; pumping up my wheelchair tires and packing up all the necessary medical equipment I might need; getting my digital camera ready with all the possible memory cards I could find as I knew I would be taking thousands of pictures and I was not sure if I could purchase memory cards over there; downloading all our personal and business passwords and files, invoices, purchase orders, contact information and banking details etc., onto our lap tops and USB flash drives, so we could deal with any issue should it arise; finding all the international plugs to take with us to convert the American 110 voltage to the 220 volt supply electricity settings in Africa; making a list of all contact phone numbers for Randa in case she needed help with the dogs or any other issue that may come up.

Now, even though we were having a heat wave in Dallas, Texas at this time, we were heading to the southern part of Africa in the southern hemisphere, where they were in the peak of winter, so we had to get all our long sleeved shirts, jerseys and sweats out of storage before we could pack.

Then, I had to notify my Aunt and Uncle that we were coming home for three weeks and ask if we could *please* stay with them! With a seven-hour time difference, I waited until midnight to call them so it was early morning over there. We were all crying on the phone at that time, from pure excitement. I am so glad that the telephones were working in Zimbabwe that morning.

We got no sleep that Wednesday night and it was already 7 am when Tammy and I realized that we had to pack and leave the house in less than an hour. It normally takes me all day just to pack for a weekend trip out of town – now we had less than an hour to pack for a three-week holiday.

We hugged and kissed our fur-kids goodbye as we hurried out the back door. It was very comforting knowing that Randa would be with them every day, loving and spoiling our boys as if they were her very own. They love their Randa.

We drove to Tammy's parents' home where we picked them up and headed to the airport. We unloaded our bags and they drove our SUV back to their house.

When we got to the counter to get our boarding passes, I also had to request that my collapsible wheelchair go into a closet on the *inside* of the cabin of the plane. The airline assistants were not sure how to handle this request and kept telling me that it had to go in the luggage compartment *under* the plane. I was insistent that it goes with me into the plane, as I have had a few experiences where the plane is taxiing away from the gate and my wheelchair is still sitting on the tarmac runway. My wheelchair is an extension of my body – they are my legs and I needed to make sure they were with me.

Finally they agreed to do this and also chose to upgrade us to business class for the first leg of our trip from Dallas to Dubai, United Arab Emirates. This was welcome news as it was a very long flight of approximately 16 hours as well as a time difference of plus nine hours!! Also, we had not slept in over 24 hours.

We had the best time on the plane – had more delicious food than we could eat, watched all the newly released movies, had foam mattresses on our huge reclining seats for a comfortable sleep and we were just treated like royalty on that flight. It was just so unreal that we were en-route home to Africa.

We landed in Dubai on Friday morning Dubai time (Thursday late night Dallas time) and had a 20-hour layover before our eight-hour connecting flight to Harare, Zimbabwe. We had a room at the airport hotel where we could shower and rest up. We were too excited to rest so we decided to spend the day wandering around Dubai. What an ordeal to get out of the airport as we had no visa to enter Dubai. Finally the nice gentleman at passport control allowed us a one-day pass to venture out of the airport. We got outside and walked towards the taxi line. We were motioned over to a line of pink taxis and informed that two women travelling alone could only travel in a taxi with a female driver – hence the pink taxis.

Our delightful driver spoke little to no English and neither one of us spoke Arabic, so…. it was a matter of drawing pictures and showing her on the map where we wanted to go. She drove us past all the magnificent buildings and told us the names of each building so we could look it up on the map and find out the history of the incredible architecture, etc. Finally we spotted the Sheraton Hotel on the beach and we asked her to drop us off there. We wanted to go to the beach and watch the sunset over the Persian Gulf.

We entered the hotel and obviously looked like tourists. The hotel staff assumed that we were staying at the hotel and directed us to their private beach. We wandered around outside and enjoyed a magnificent sunset and some appetizers and soft drinks on this beautiful section of beach. After a few hours, we left there and returned to the international airport hotel. We showered and wandered around the duty free shops until it was time to board our next flight.

Once again I had to convince them to take my collapsible wheelchair into the cabin with me. Even though we were not upgraded into business class on this flight, we were still treated like first class passengers in the economy section of Emirates Airlines. It was brilliant.

As we arrived in Harare, Zimbabwe on Saturday evening we experienced a magnificent sunset from the plane. As soon as we entered the airport building all the lights went out. No Power. Welcome to Zimbabwe where no electricity is common-place! Everyone else carried on as normal and all I could see were the oversized whites of Tammy's eyes staring at me. It was the start of an amazing adventure. With no power, it took a little while for our bags to be manually removed from the plane before we could leave the building.

Waiting outside for us were my Uncle Salvo and cousin Twinny. It was totally overwhelming to see them. We hugged, loaded our bags and headed to a suburb called Groomsbridge, outside of the major capital city of Harare (formerly called Salisbury). There we were loved and hugged on by my Auntie Lila and other cousin Nonees, the one I was skyping with just four days earlier. We also had the pleasure of meeting their maid and our new friend Sitabelli. No words can truly express the emotions that both Tammy and I were feeling at this time. I had last seen my Aunt and Uncle in Dallas three years earlier when they stayed with us in Plano while visiting with my Mom (Auntie Lila's only sibling) before she passed away. I had not seen my cousins for about 18 years – they were now living in the neighbouring country of South Africa and were back in Zimbabwe for their Dad's birthday celebration.

It was a shock for Tammy to experience many hours/days of no electricity or running water. It was not too much of an issue for me, even though I had become spoilt by living in the USA where we take electricity and running water so for granted. Out of necessity, my family has a generator for power and a plastic storage tank for water on their property. Even so, pouring water out of a one-gallon tank into the toilet so we could flush, took some getting used to.

Celebrating his 80th birthday.
(l-r) Fortunee, Auntie Lila, Linda and Uncle Salvo. *Zimbabwe*

The next day, Sunday was actually Uncle Salvo's birthday and we got together with about 50 of their friends and celebrated over a fabulous lunchtime meal. I was delighted to be able to read my own speech, in person, to my Uncle.

The following day I got to see Dazie and Sonia, two of my best friends for the past 40 plus years. The next two weeks were filled with very little sleep as we crammed in all the sights. Lots of walks down memory lane; visiting my previous homes, my junior and high schools, my previous places of employment; our supermarkets and butcheries; petrol stations; movie houses; the tobacco auction floors; the malls and our favourite hang-out places; the local food and clothing markets and the sports clubs where I played field hockey and squash. We enjoyed delicious meals with family and friends, attended a live theatre production, made new friends and spent some time in the bush, away from the city.

The majestic Victoria Falls. *Zimbabwe*

We took a one-hour flight on a small 60 seater airplane and were able to visit one of my most favourite places in the universe, the Victoria Falls. There, we went on a photographic safari, where we saw African elephants, rhinoceros (both the black and white species), giraffes, hippopotamus, buffalo, zebra (donkeys in pyjamas), gorillas, chimpanzees, baboons, monkeys (branch managers), crocodiles, wild dogs, hyenas, warthogs, wildebeest and herds of sable antelope, waterbuck, impala, kudu, eland and many varieties of various African birds. We did not get to see any of the "big cats" on this trip, lions, leopards or cheetahs.

We enjoyed many hours wandering around the five falls that collectively make up the Victoria Falls. We enjoyed seeing several, super vivid double rainbows; getting wet from the towering columns of spray from the massive amounts of falling water; interacting with lots of small game animals; watching the steam train travel across into Zambia; admiring the rickety Zambezi river bridge all while hearing the thunderous noise of the Victoria Falls, one of the Seven natural Wonders of the World.

We rode on a rescued African elephant named Hwange, enjoyed hours of local entertainment including music and dancing and ate lots of local foods. This was an absolutely culinary delight for me and I was so excited that Tammy was willing to try all the local foods including mopane worms. We got to visit with the local witch doctor, who would throw the bones to read our fortunes and we relaxed on a sunset cruise on the Zambezi river where we got to watch an elephant crossing over from Zambia to Zimbabwe. It was amazing to see just the elephant's trunk sticking out of the water as she crossed the river.

**Hwange took Tammy, myself and Rodney for a ride
in the African Bush.** *Zimbabwe*

Besides being with my family and friends, the most soul quenching and spirit revitalizing part of this entire trip for me was re-visiting the world's biggest baobab tree at Victoria Falls. I am unsure of my spiritual connection with this particular tree and yet there is something magical and unexplainable that I feel when I am near the baobab tree.

This tree is believed to be between 1,000 and 1,500 years old, stands over 75 feet tall and has a circumference of about 60 feet. The bottom of the tree has messages carved into it from the 1800's. The native legend surrounding this tree is that the G-ds were angry, so they pulled the tree up by the roots and put it back in the ground upside down, hence the branches looks like roots. The fruit of this tree is used to make cream-of-tarter.

My inspiration and spiritual connection, the baobab tree. *Zimbabwe*

Seeing everything through the eyes of a first-timer to Africa was amazing. There were so many things I was used to seeing and totally understood and yet they were so very foreign to Tammy. A few in particular come to mind – The African women carry their infant children around on their backs, held on with a towel wrapped around the women's waist; These same women also carry almost everything on their heads, wood for fires, buckets of water, bags of food, etc. She commented regularly on the super friendly attitude and mild mannered gentle energy of the local people. Tammy was also amazed at the close distance of the sun and the moon and the stars, feeling like she could reach out and touch them. It was a delightful and wonderful experience to see my home through her eyes.

I hope you got to enjoy our trip to Africa as much as we did. This is just another reason to believe that anything and everything is possible.

Thanks to Rob and Joy for your love and generosity and for making this dream trip a reality for us. Thanks also to Auntie Lila and Uncle Salvo, Uncle Alvin and Auntie Sarah, Twinny, Nonees, Dazie, Sonia, Ginny, Annie and Sitabelli for making this another trip of a lifetime for us.

...and to think that after "My Opportunity," it was highly recommended that I spend the rest of my life in a fully assisted nursing home....WOW... so that is how the cow ate the cabbage!

**Tammy and I had our fortunes read by this witch doctor
at The Boma.** *Zimbabwe*

Openings in Heaven

When my mother, who was my first and best friend, passed away in 2010 it was the hardest thing I ever had to deal with. No one is really ever prepared for the death of a loved one and even though my parents were in their early 80's and they were ill and tired, it was still a very painful and emotional time for us. Dad passed away in 2004 surrounded by all his loving family. We were so lucky to have Mom live with Tammy and me for about two years before she passed away at home. She died in my arms with Tammy, Skippy and Nano holding us close together.

Then, in the summer of 2014, my brother Mikey who was only 63, passed away and I certainly was not prepared for his death either. Selfishly, I wanted Mikey to stay in this world and yet with the excruciating pain and suffering he was enduring, I did a lot of soul searching and arrived at a place of acceptance. He had a drastically diminished quality of life and was just existing, so I asked that G-D do *His Will* - heal him so he could walk out of the hospital whole and healthy again or take him to heaven where he could be free of pain and suffering and rest in peace.

I am grateful for all the terrific times we spent together, for all the hugs, tears and laughs we shared throughout our lives and now for all the amazing memories I hold dear in my heart.

We all have our own individual paths to travel during our time on this planet, and often our paths cross or intertwine with another person's journey and yet ultimately, the path we travel is just a single, one-way lane. Our time to go *or* our time to stay is just that...our time! We don't know our expiration date so make a daily choice to see the best in everything and everyone and celebrate each day like it's your last.

Grieving is such a personal matter with no right or wrong way to do it and no time frame in which to handle and process this emotion. My grief for the loss of my loved ones is purely selfish – I want them physically here with me where I can hug them, laugh with them, hold them, cook for them, kiss them, talk with them, drive with them, share with them, eat with them, get advice from them, cruise with them, phone them, cuss and discuss with them and so much more. On an unselfish level, I know they are happier, healed and whole again in Heaven. I have no regrets and no remorse over what I *could have* done or *should have* done (no woulda, coulda, shoulda) and for me, this makes my grieving process a little easier with no anger and bitterness to deal with.

When I look up at the night-sky, I often wonder if the stars are really just little openings in heaven that allow our loved ones to smile down on us.

British/African English *When I Say this...*	American/Texas English *I Mean this:*
American football	Football
Anti-clockwise	Counter-clockwise
Avocado pear	Avocado
Bangers	Sausages
Belt up	Shut up
Beetroot	Beets
Biscuit (chocolate chip)	Cookie
Bloke	Guy
Bloody	Very (used to emphasize)
Bonnet of a car	Hood of a car
Boot of a car	Trunk of a car
Braai	BBQ
Braces	Suspenders
Brackets	Parentheses
Bum	Butt / fanny
Butt	Filter of a cigarette
Car park	Parking lot
Cheeky	Flippant
Cheerio	Good-bye
Cheque	Check
Chips	French fries
Chuffed	Pleased
Cot	Crib
Cubby hole (car)	Console
Cupboard	Closet
Dim	Stupid

British/African English *When I Say this...*	American/Texas English *I Mean this:*
Donkey's years	Ages / long time
Dress smart	Get dressed up
Dummy	Pacifier
Engaged (telephone)	Busy signal
Fall pregnant	Get pregnant
Fishing rod	Fishing pole
Flat	Apartment
Football	Soccer
Fortnight	Two weeks
Full of beans	Lots of energy
Full stop	Period
Give way sign	Yield sign
Gobsmacked	Astounded / astonished
Gown	Robe
Handbag	Purse
Hand basin	Sink
Hang around	Piddle around
Hold on	Stop or wait
Holiday	Vacation
Hose pipe	Water hose
Ice-lollies	Popsicles
Jam	Jelly
Jelly	Jell-O
Jolly good / nice	Very good / nice
Just now	In a little while
Lift	Elevator

British/African English	American/Texas English
When I Say this...	*I Mean this:*
Loo / toilet	Restroom / bathroom
Lorry	Truck
Mealie	Corn
Mind out	Watch out / be careful
Mootie	Medicine
Nappy	Diaper
Not my cup of tea	Not to my liking
Opening mootie	Laxative
Pavement	Sidewalk
Peckish	Slightly hungry
Period	Menstrual cycle
Petrol	Gas
Piddle	Pee / urinate
Piece of cake	Easy to do
Pips	Seeds
Poppy cock	Nonsense
Purse	Wallet
Pushchair	Stroller
Queue	Line
Randy	Horny
Reverse charges	Call collect
Return trip	Round trip
Row	Argument
Rubbish	Garbage / trash
Rubbish bin/dust bin	Garbage / trash can
Robots	Traffic lights

British/African English *When I Say this...*	American/Texas English *I Mean this:*
Rubber	Eraser or condom
Scone	Biscuit
Serviette	Napkin
Smart	Well dressed
Spanner	Wrench
Spend a penny	Go to the bathroom
Stretcher	Gurney
Stroke	Slash
Surname	Last name
Swear	Curse / cuss
Sweets	Candies
Swimming costume	Swimsuit
Takkies	Track shoes
Take away	Take out
Tap	Faucet
Tea (hot tea)	Iced tea
Theatre	Operating / surgery room
Tomato sauce	Ketchup
Torch	Flashlight
Vagina	Fanny
Verandah	Patio
Windscreen	Windshield
Wonky	Unstable
Zed (last letter of the alphabet)	Zee

Epilogue

Thank you for reading my stories, sharing my experiences and travelling beside me on this journey. I want to share this book with as many people as possible, so that they may become their own catalyst for change. I want to encourage them to look inside themselves and become empowered, thereby creating a continual process of positive changes for themselves which will ultimately have an amazing ripple effect of positive changes for our beautiful world.

This book has been a work in progress over several years and recently, the pre-publication editing, presented its own set of opportunities. Due to my vision and memory challenges, it has been a very long process for me to read each of my short stories, edit the information, while remembering the point of that particular story! I have amnesia and deja vu at the same time – I think I have forgotten this before.

This past year alone has been one of those years in which I could have easily been sucked into the big black hole of despair, doom and gloom. I am sharing this so that when you read this book, you too can know that it is possible to get through the darkest times in your life. Just when you think that everything is falling apart in your life, perhaps the pieces are really just falling into place! It is possible to turn every apparent disaster into a blessing and an opportunity.

This is one of my greatest personal accomplishments confirming the deep realization I feel, of how I have evolved and changed since the start of "My Opportunity."

Each story has a moral and/or life lesson that I have learnt and continue to benefit from. I continue to grow each and every day, as I hope you choose to do after reading some of my experiences, so we can all continue to "RideStrong through Life's Journey."

Be the change you wish to see in the world.
– Mahatma Gandhi

Please feel free to email me at RideStrong@aol.com
and visit my website, www.DebLewin.com

Thanks to Owen at U-Edit Video for designing my logo.
www.ueditvideo.com

About Deb Lewin

In her many years of riding, Deb has accomplished many goals as an Equestrian and all of this on borrowed horses. She qualified at IPEC Competitions and was selected to compete in two Paralympic trials in dressage (top 10 riders in the USA); She has been a medal winning member of the USA ParaEquestrian team for international dressage competition; Deb has won the title of UPHA national champion and reserve national champion in equitation; Deb was the recipient of the Equest Levi Strauss award and was voted as the NARHA (now PATH) independent equestrian of the year.

Deb is the proud owner of several large trophies and shiny belt buckles from the AQHA for year-end high point awards in both English and Western disciplines and has won or placed in numerous local and national competitions for both able-bodied and challenged riders, sometimes even taking high point of the show awards. Deb has received the Dallas Cowboy's Community Quarterback Award for volunteering from the Gene and Jerry Jones Family Charities. She has received the Dallas North Star Award and has been inducted into the Equest Hall of Fame.

When Deb is not in the saddle, she volunteers to share her story about the phenomenal horses she has had the pleasure of being with and the amazing benefits of therapeutic riding. She shares stories about the benefits of having a positive attitude, sense of humour and how she has overcome so many challenges and embraced her difficulties. Deb knows that life can be tough and she definitely knows that she is tougher. She speaks with groups large and small, people young and old, able-bodied or alternatively-abled like herself. She encourages everyone she meets, to

"RideStrong Through Life's Journey!"

Tammy and I are from opposite ends of the world and it works! *Texas*

*"Your living is determined not so much by what life brings to you
as by the attitude you bring to life;
not so much by what happens to you
as by the way your mind looks at what happens."*
- Kahlil Gibran

For personally autographed copies or to obtain the audio version of this book visit:

www.DebLewin.com

Please contact Deb Lewin if you would like her to be your Guest Speaker or Inspirational Story Teller at:

Your Next Event,
Company Meetings,
Corporate Functions,
Banquets,
Conferences or
Non-profits Special Events

~

Follow Deb on Facebook

A portion of the profits from the sale of each book will be donated to Equest Therapeutic Horsemanship in Wylie, Texas. Equest is a non-profit organization that offers equine assisted therapy to children and adults with physical and mental disabilities as well as equine programmes for Veterans and their families.

The monies donated through the sale of this book will go towards the Deb Lewin Scholoarship fund. This scholarship programme offers financial assistance to current Equest riders to help offset the expenses associated with participating in horse shows and to assist staff members towards fees for continuing education.

Made in the USA
Charleston, SC
19 December 2014